Secrets
of
Dating After Fifty

*The Insider's Guide to
Finding Love Again*

Karen Haddigan

in collaboration with Debi Helm

ISBN: 978-1-7323831-0-4
KDsays Publishing
Santa Barbara, CA

Cover Design by Damonza
Illustrations by Damonza

Library of Congress Control Number: 2018911799

NOTE: All the stories in this book are true.
Some details have been changed to protect
identities. (Otherwise, they'd have to kill us!)

"Dating after 50 is easy.
It's like riding a bike.
But the bike is on fire.
And the ground is on fire.
Everything is on fire.
Because you are in hell."

—Author Unknown

Contents

Preface

How We Got Here

*I*T ALL STARTED when my friend Debi went on a coffee date, hoping this might be "the one." They'd texted and talked on the phone, where she sensed the first stirrings of excitement. As soon as she saw him, she felt a connection. He looked even better than his photos. The caffeine and conversation flowed. She smiled a lot; so did he. It wasn't like other first dates.

They talked easily and for much longer than it took to drink a cup of coffee—about themselves, their lives, what they were each looking for. Tender strands of attraction started to form.

Later, saying goodbye at her car, he pulled her in and

kissed her gently. They both knew something big was starting. The next morning, he texted her. "Good morning. I really liked meeting you, you're very special." She texted him, "Thank you and yes, very special connection." He: "I have to go out of town on business tomorrow. Let's get together for lunch when I get back." She: "I would love lunch."

She never heard from him again.

Debi and I had both started online dating, and over time we'd developed a kind of "buddy debriefing system." Together, we deconstructed the problem of the day, mostly while trudging up our favorite hiking trail.

I'd experienced similar situations. We both felt like clueless teenagers, full of questions with no answers and mystified about how we were supposed to figure out dating again at this age.

Debi is in her early fifties, I'm in my mid-sixties and while our life journeys have been very different, the origins of this particular mystery tour into late-in-life dating were remarkably similar.

Almost ten years ago, each of us arrived in impossibly perfect Santa Barbara with its perfect weather and its movie-set Spanish village architecture. I was married and ecstatic to be abandoning the oppressive rain forest that was Seattle for my lifelong dream of living in California.

Debi was engaged and had left the cold and windy city of Chicago with her fiancé for this idyllic little West Coast town.

Arriving in Santa Barbara with our life partners was like landing at heaven's door—a sleepy yet vibrant community nestled by the ocean and framed by a gentle mountain range, with graceful palm trees, a balmy Mediterranean climate, and beaches that went on for miles. What could go wrong?

But it did. We'll spare you the rant and the gory details about what happened to those relationships—the deterioration, the wounds, and the pain—if you've suffered a break-up, you know the drill, and it sucks.

The life I'd been living was gone. Suddenly, there was no one to look up at when I was reading and say, "Honey, listen to this." No one to eat with, take a road trip with, snuggle up on the couch with. I went to therapy and every meditation group I could get my hands on, letting the tears roll while I sat in silent contemplation. I bought books on emotional healing and binge-watched old episodes of *The Gilmore Girls* in the middle of the afternoon in my PJs.

Debi's plans of a wedding at a luxurious hillside resort morphed into a new life as an *Uber* driver to make ends meet. With a daughter in high school, the idea of failing and having to leave Santa Barbara was not an option.

After years of being homeowners, we both became renters again. Old friends, mostly couples, drifted away. The fall from grace included losing our lifestyles, our previous identities, and half our assets.

But as with most stories, endings signal new beginnings, and eventually we picked up the broken pieces of our lives, put our big-girl pants on, and started over. Deciding to date again was part of that journey. However, after decades in relationships, we found that the dating world had changed radically and we were standing there like *Alice in Wonderland*, surrounded by mad hatters and white rabbits, and more than a little stunned.

It's not that we're naïve. Between us, we've been married, divorced, widowed, in long-term relationships and short-term relationships. We've each met previous partners online. We're both mothers and grandmothers. Debi was widowed with three small children before she was forty. I was a single mother for years.

In short, we've been around the block a few times, but this modern dating thing made us scratch our heads. Over time, we've met many other fifty-plus singles who are perplexed and frustrated. This includes men, whose questions and complaints were very much like ours.

It's not only that we're all required now to have sparkling online personas and Twitter accounts that are linked to our Instagrams and our Facebooks for reasons we don't understand, but our minds and bodies aren't the shiny pennies they used to be. Dating someone at this age isn't about meeting the parents or making babies, but it *is* about excess baggage, chemistry, texting, old-body sex, and OMG so much more.

The final spark that propelled us forward was when one of Debi's dates told her that before he started dating again after his divorce, he searched for a book to help, but couldn't find one.

We've now been out there dating for a while and believe we have a handle on some of its conundrums. Our skins are thicker, we've learned new skills, and thanks to our friendship, we have somebody to turn to when life goes weird, as it often does.

The way we figure it, if we share our secrets and screw-ups, maybe you won't have to slide quite as far down the rabbit hole as we did at first. If you're divorced or widowed and over fifty, you have enough to handle.

Dating is more art than science, though. You will get better with practice, but if you're looking for a guarantee you'll find that one perfect person, put down your pencil.

If, however, you're looking for some guidance, support, tips, and a few laughs, we've got your back. You may or may not meet the last love of your life, but if you give dating a try, at the very least, you're in for an adventure!

Are You Ready For This?

*I'm not interested in online dating.
I'd rather stick with good old-fashioned
alcohol and poor judgment.*

— Author Unknown

On Your Own Again

AH, THE SINGLE life. More alone time than you ever dreamed possible. Cruising the streets for 7:30 movies and eating cold pizza in front of the TV. On the upside, the closet is all yours; so is the bed.

Not what you had in mind?

You may want to run right out and replace that somebody you lost with another somebody. But before you do, you gotta gotta gotta go through the grieving process. It hurts like crazy, and you may be tempted to skip over it and bury those feelings somewhere in the backyard, but if you don't give grieving the time and work it demands, it'll come back and bite you in whatever next relationship you try to have.

Some of the work involves soul-searching about our part in the issues from our previous relationships. Whether you're divorced, widowed, or just crawled out of a cave, a little reflection and self-responsibility go a long way toward making you better next time around. What bad behavior did you engage in? What did you learn about yourself in the relationship? What responsibility do you take for the issues that came between you and your partner? (There's a quiz coming up. NOT!)

If you're feeling mopey and stuck, this quote from noted scholar and author Joseph Campbell might help:

"We must be willing to get rid of the life we've planned, so as to have the life that is waiting for us."

And that's the thing: you thought it was all going to work out one way and it didn't, so it's time to move along and find out what else life has in store for you. Being forced into change and new opportunities is life giving us a chance to become more of who we really are. I recently ran into an eighty-year-old woman who is dating an eighty-five-year-old man. She says she is only now realizing this is the first time she truly feels like herself in a relationship.

Who Are You, Anyway?

If you've been part of a couple for years, when it ends you're limping around like half a person for a while. You've negotiated and compromised, and now that you don't have to, you have to re-learn yourself.

And who you are will change. The you who existed in that couple is not you anymore. The parts you repressed to get along, the parts you overdeveloped, all the ways you twisted and bent and adapted—no longer needed.

Contemplate. Ruminate. Take time to work on your stuff. Too many people jump into a new relationship only to have to go through yet another break-up because they tried to skip a step. Or, as Ginette Paris says in her book *Heartbreak*,

> *"Do not plug any new relationship into the old socket of your past wounding."*

It doesn't hurt to find some other single friends to hang out with in the meantime. Take some classes. Join something. Take up a new activity. Volunteer. Check out the local Meet-up groups. (You may not know what those are. Google it.)

Humans need contact with other humans, and living alone sucks sometimes—but then so does living with someone you can't stand. Then all you want is to be left alone. Yes, there will be sobbing and the gnashing of teeth after a break-up or death, but there will also be the flowering of a new you. Watch for it.

OK, Done Grieving. How Do I Meet Someone?

When you were married or otherwise coupled, you probably didn't pay much attention to all those people in Starbucks with their heads down, intently swiping left and right on their cell phones, but just so you know, they're dating. Or more accurately, they're judging a person's attractiveness based on one earnest, hopeful photo with an age and geographic location next to it and rejecting or accepting said person with a casual brush of a finger while sipping their non-fat soy lattes. If you noticed, you likely thought something like, *Thank God I don't have to do that anymore.*

And then shit happened. Somebody died, somebody cheated, somebody left somebody and there you were. Single, not ready for the rocking chair, but where on Earth do you meet a new potential partner?

You've probably realized that at this age, you're not likely to find the next love of your life in a bar, the gym, or the produce section at Trader Joe's anymore, although you are welcome to try. Good luck with that.

Or, you might be considering the "friend fix-up" method. Some of you may be lucky enough to have that mythical friend who knows the perfect person for you, sets you up on a date, and bam! You live happily ever after without missing a beat. By the way, if you happen to have any friends like that, please send them over.

Here's the deal: online dating is how it's done now, and we all might as well get used to it. Yes, yes, the whole idea of packaging yourself online to meet someone sounds like about as much fun as having your fingernails ripped out, and at our age (wherever you are on the scale from fifty to dead), life has already had quite enough challenges. But online dating does provide some improvements over old-school ways to meet someone.

So let's say you were to hang out for hours at the grocery store (or the bar, or the gym) every day in hopes of accidentally running into the man or woman of your dreams; you will never encounter the number of people that a dating site will serve up to your laptop or phone screen. It's highly convenient and a little creepy, like shopping for a person—although not as creepy as lurking in public places hoping to lure a stranger to your house.

Another advantage of online dating is you have some information about the person before you make contact (unlike meeting someone in a bar, where you know nothing except they're cute and they drink alcohol).

It can also be exciting, like a kid in a candy shop. So many choices, right at your fingertips. Put in your basic criteria and up pops seventeen pages of potentials. Press a key and choose the perfect person... Go ahead enjoy that thought for a moment. You done? OK, because it doesn't work like that. It should, but it doesn't.

Most people who do online dating have a love/hate relationship with it. While fun and exciting, online dating requires stamina, a thick skin, and the ability to make an accurate assessment of a person's soul from a photo and an idealized self-description—which is impossible. This means you'll likely go on dates with people you never should've. Still, it's practice.

How Long Should You Wait to Date?

I was in the middle of my divorce when I first went online and looked at a few dating sites, but they just made me cry. When you're bereft and grieving, there's nothing more depressing than looking at a bunch of hopeful photos of old people waiting to date you. So I went back to grieving and meditating and therapy for a while.

On the other hand, some of us are ready the minute we (or our partner) walk out the door. We did most of our grieving during the unraveling of the relationship. In that case, screw the waiting thing and get out there. You're not getting any younger. But the previous comments about self-reflection still apply, so at least take a deep breath first.

Shortly after the end of Debi's seven-year relationship, her daughters said something to the effect of, "Mom, you're young, you're vibrant, you have to get out there." They grabbed her laptop and wrote her profile. Not to limit her possibilities, they said, "I love everything except cilantro" (she's allergic). They dug up photos, grabbed her credit card, and signed mom up on a few sites. And off she went. They had to kick the little birdie out of the nest and force her to fly.

Get in Shape!

The comfort of a long-term relationship can easily devolve us into mushy little couch potatoes over the course of many years. Your previous partner loved you with that spare tire you sprouted bit by bit, conspiring with you in those late-night runs to buy chocolate chip cookie mix, but re-entering the dating world means you're being looked at with eyes that don't include decades of devotion and sweet memories of your hot twenty- or thirty-something self.

We all have to accept gravity, muscle loss, and wrinkles (the list is longer but let's not overwhelm ourselves here). The simple concept is that your physical state makes a difference in whether and how many people will find you attractive. Your stellar personality and formidable wit come later.

Right now it's time to take an honest appraisal, assess eating and lifestyle habits, check with your doctor about your overall health and then hit the gym, get on that bike, or pull out that exerciser contraption you bought from an infomercial years ago—you know, the one that's under the bed, covered in dust bunnies. And no, you can't count golf as an exercise regimen.

It's not simply about looking good. You may have developed some minor (or major) aches and pains from surfing that sofa or sitting in front of all those screens for years. Getting in shape helps us look better and can relieve ailments and increase energy levels, so that we're not gasping or limping along on that romantic beach walk that everybody wistfully yearns for in their online dating profiles.

Also, how about updating your look? Have you changed your haircut, your glasses, or your style of dress since the '90s—hell, the '70s? Do you still wear tightie whities with holes in them or granny panties with failing elastic? Are your jeans hiked all the way up to your waist? Oh wait, that's been out of style for so long that it's coming back in again.

Are You Willing to Put in the Time?

It's worth saying that the people who are the most successful at dating put effort into it. It's like a part-time job, requiring attention and commitment.

Every step works better if you take time with it—from photos to profiles to messaging people and dating behavior. If you're just going to dabble, or if you expect the right person to show up quickly and without much effort on your part, you are either impossibly good-looking, charismatic, or rich (and even then, look how long it took George Clooney to find Amal). Think marathon, not sprint. Needle in haystack, not smorgasbord.

Who Are Your People?

Okay, let's get into it. If you're not familiar with the online dating sites, you may not know there are a gazillion of them, and some cater to very specific needs, desires, and types of people. There's a hodgepodge of lifestyles out there. Whether you're hetero, gay, bi, or something else, you can drill down to find "your people." Some examples:

- Polyamorous
- Fetishes
- Sugar daddies
- Trans
- Geeks
- Farmers
- Clowns (just put this in here to check if you were paying attention, but it's a real thing)
- Pet owners
- Over-50 crowd
- Affluent/Elite
- Highly attractive
- Famous or near-famous
- Religion-based

There are many more categories; we're just giving you

the general flavor here. Even if you're not a geek-farmer-clown with a fetish who's looking for a sugar daddy, there are many sites to choose from, and more pop up all the time. If you don't know how to find them, start by Googling "online dating." You can also stick in "mature singles" or other catchy, senior-like phrases to help narrow your search.

Some dating sites rely heavily on photographs (stay away from those sites if you're over fifty, unless you somehow look like you're thirty-five), while others ask for extensive profiles and/or offer questionnaires. And while the idea of having to write an essay about yourself and your hugely imperfect life can be enough to keep you avoiding your laptop for weeks, both pics and profiles are important and you'll have to do them. We'll help.

We're not recommending any particular sites. They each have their advantages and disadvantages—numbers of subscribers, ease of navigation on the pages, amount of information about a person, questionnaires or not, etc., and more appear every day.

What Kind of Relationship Do You Want?

Once you've figured out if you're a vanilla or specialty-category dater, the sites will ask about the kind of relationship you're looking for. Just friends? Travel partner? Pen pal? Long-term commitment? Marriage? Personal assistant? Live-in cook? (Kidding with those last two—you knew that, right?)

Beyond the labels, consider what kind of relationship makes sense for you at this stage of life. Many of us have already experienced what we consider the love of our life, so then what? Is it possible to have two important loves in this lifetime or do we only get one chance at the big wheel?

Check your beliefs before you limit yourself. Deep love can and does happen at this stage of life; sometimes it's just a matter of being open to it.

There are people (both men and women) who ask for something called "friends first," which might be their way of trying to avoid the one-night stands, or it could mean something else. We assume it means that hanky-panky will be waaaaay down the road.

Or not. I have a friend who met a woman who stated she was looking for a "friends first" relationship, so he respectfully kept his hands to himself, and then she promptly jumped his bones on the third date. Which goes to show you that people are complicated, and we don't always know what we want—or mean what we say.

If you're not sure what you want, don't specify, or check all the boxes but *do* expect that anyone you meet or talk to will likely ask you what kind of relationship you're looking for. Don't assume that people are all looking for that one special person, or partner, or spouse. Some just wanna have fun.

I was on a first date with a guy who casually mentioned that he was currently seeing another woman, so after choking quietly on my coffee, I gathered up my cool and "casually" asked him how she felt about him being on a dating site. He said she knew and it was fine.

I assumed they had a casual, non-exclusive relationship and that he was looking for something more serious, but then it came out that the other relationship had been going on for a year and although she lived out of town, she stayed with him several days a week. I didn't bother to stick around to find out how many days he was trying to fill with a second woman. Buh-bye.

To Pay or Not to Pay

Many sites are free when they first come on the scene, until they get enough subscribers. Then they usually become a site you have to pay to use. And while many sites will let you browse with some limitations before you decide to join, they usually make you submit a photo and a profile before you can see profiles of other subscribers.

Look around before you decide which one to join. Many people join more than one to increase the possibilities.

Once you've found a site or sites you like and are ready to sign up, you have to pick a time period. They'll offer discounts if you join for a longer time, but you might find you don't like the site after a short while and there are no refunds, so in that way, it's better to choose the shorter time period at first until you find out which one works best for you.

Most sites have a variety of add-ons they'll try to sell you. These include features like paying extra so you can sneak around and look at profiles without the person knowing or being able to find out when a person has opened your message. We suggest you leave these features alone at first until you understand how the sites work and what you need.

Advice from the Dating Sites

Most dating sites come complete with advice, and much of it, in our humble opinion, sucks. For example, one site advises you to "emphasize your accomplishments." I'm sorry but I'm not interested in your resume; I want to date you, not hire you.

Another site suggests you'll be more likely to get responses if you use the word "nice" in your message to someone online. *Nice profile? Nice pics? Nice day?* Really?

Dating sites also offer bland, say-nothing generic profile

suggestions that make anyone sound, well, bland and generic. (More help on page 23 and the Appendix for how to write a profile that expresses your personality.)

On the other hand, the dating sites offer advice on safety, which is a good thing. So go ahead and read through their advice, but use your own judgment about what's going to help or not.

Wait, Wait! One More Thing Before You Run Out There

STDs (sexually transmitted diseases): Sorry to take the air out of your balloon, but we've gotta talk about it and so will you.

You might've been in a monogamous relationship for years, but others you meet haven't, so decide before you even start dating how you're going to handle this. It's common for people you date to expect you to get tested for STDs before agreeing to have sex, so be prepared.

At the very least, own up to anything you are bringing to the party and hope like hell they do, too. Use protection if you're not sure. More about this later on page 98. For now, 'nuff said. You're a grown-up.

Assembling Your Virtual Self

*"I love dating strangers from the
Internet - Said no one, ever."*

—Author Unknown

*U*NLIKE THE OLD days when you'd meet a
person in a non-dating environment, get to
know them a bit, and then maybe go on a
date, in the online world all you have is a photo, a profile,
and a username. It's not much to go on, but it's all you've
got to capture someone's attention. So it's everything.

Photos

Moment of truth here. This aspect of online dating is a bitch for those of us over fifty, more so for those of us over sixty. Skin has weathered, hair has receded or disappeared altogether, crinkles and wrinkles and graying and bulges that didn't used to be there are now threatening to cramp our "Never getting old 'cuz I'm a Boomer" style.

But it is what it is, and it's why the older among us tend to prefer dating sites based on more than a quick swipe across a photo.

Regarding pics, more is better, so be prepared with at least three or four. More photos equal more attention. But let's face it: no matter how many photos you have, the younger and more classically attractive you are, the more responses you're likely to get.

Your photo is the first thing others see, and many people will accept or reject you based on that alone. Find or take some pictures in a variety of settings or events or activities. We can't do what younger people do online: post a hot selfie and everybody comes running. Besides, you're not just looking for a hot date, right? Right?

Some people advise using professional photographers for profile pics, but the way we figure it, you should always look better in real life, and professional photos usually make you look AH-mazing. Your 3-D self shouldn't be a disappointment from your online self, which is also a warning not to play around with the photo-editing software to get rid of those bags under your eyes. It's tempting, we know.

Some Do's and Don'ts About Photos:

- DO NOT use old photos. The more recent, the better. Brutal honesty here: even one-year-old pics at this age can be quite different from how you look now. Also, nobody cares about your prom pictures, or the ones from thirty years ago when you were a hippie or a rising sports star. It's really great you used to be so handsome or beautiful, but that was then and this is now, so get rid of those.

- Avoid blurred, darkly lit, and far-away pics. This seems obvious, right? You wouldn't believe how many people do all of the above. We know they're hiding something—that, or else they're not trying very hard. Special note to the dudes: please please please stop with the endless pics of you in a baseball cap and sunglasses. And that includes photos of you skiing, complete with a hat pulled down over your entire head, ears, and forehead, plus huge goggles and a bulky snow suit.

- Play up your assets, but don't attempt to hide your bad features or your size. Your date will get the full picture as soon as they meet you and you'll disappoint them and the date will be a disaster and there goes another day of your life.

  Include at least one full-length shot; lots and lots of people—men and women—try to hide their weight by showing only head shots. Or were you planning to show up to the first date with only your head?

- Make sure you're smiling and looking at the camera in your main photo, so you look friendly and not like a psycho killer. Actually, do more than that. When so much is riding on a picture, an inviting face is key. We can't stress this enough.

  When we are flipping through the multitude of online photos, we scour them for what we've dubbed "friendly eyes," and those are the ones we are drawn to. The look you want is best achieved by imagining someone you really really love when your picture is being taken, not by thinking, *Oh God, I'm going to advertise myself on the Internet.*

- Try to avoid selfies. News flash: selfies make your nose look big. Plus, it looks like you have no friends. Maybe have a good friend or family member take some photos of you, if you don't have good recent ones.

- The creepiest version of the selfie are those too-frequent bathroom mirror ones. Frankly, they look exactly like what they are—you, locked in a bathroom alone with a camera, staring at yourself.

- And we couldn't leave this topic without mentioned the car selfies, taken with your phone in that convenient holder that photographs you from below, so we can all enjoy the visual delight of looking up your nostrils and admiring your double chin.

- Women, don't throw your boobies out there unless sex is your goal. Guys love looking and you'll get a lot of attention, but you'll spend your time on the date saying, "My eyes are up here," a lot.

- Men, please keep your shirt on. We really don't want to see your chest until we know you better. And seriously guys, no dick pics. We get that you're proud of it but keep it in your pants for now, okay?

- Pets and children or grandchildren. One photo of you with your significant others is great, but don't be that person who has one pic of themselves, and a gajillion of their entire gene pool of offspring and their dog doing cute pet tricks.

- Scenery. Maybe you live in a beautiful place or you love flowers. Save it for your profile and make the pics about what you look like. This also goes for pics of your hot car, ancient buildings from your tour of Europe, and that painting of a sunset you recently finished.

- Group photos. We can't tell you how many times people use group photos without telling us which one you are. To you, it's obvious. To strangers on the Internet, not so much.

- You and your toys. If you have a nice yacht or a private plane and you show it off, you'll tend to attract a stream of sugar daddy/mama hopefuls, so tone it down.

- Think outside the box. Don't have every picture of yourself in the same room wearing the same clothes, sitting in the same chair. Different settings and different activities show us a more rounded version of who you are.

- Pay attention to what else appears in the photo. How are you dressed? Who and what else is in the photo and what does it say about who you are? I mean, who wouldn't love to date a person whose photos feature their half-eaten breakfast and a dead plant in the background?

- Check your photos after you post them on the dating site. There are lots of profile pics out there featuring corners of rooms and headless torsos.

One final note: some people attempt to go online without photos. Not a good choice. We avoid those people like the plague, and assume they're up to no good, even if they're really shy or are afraid to be seen online. We figure they are married, fake, or the ever-worrisome psycho killer.

Profiles

Profiles are those mini-essays that most sites ask you to write about yourself. Ugh, right? But it's gotta be done. The first line of your profile is arguably the most important, because people are looking at lots and lots of profiles and besides, we all have internet-damaged attention spans.

Spend the most time on that first line and think of it as marketing yourself, because that's what it is. You want to capture the eye of the roving reader, so say something unique. There's a sameness to many profiles and soon it all sounds like blah blah blah sunsets, blah blah blah cuddling in front of a fire, blah blah blah no drama, please.

Your profile is a chance for someone to start getting to know your personality. It's not only about the facts.

We're not as interested in what you've done, as in what you believe, what excites you, what you have to offer a partner, how you spend your time. Read other profiles if you're stumped about what to say. Which ones stand out to you? But resist the urge to use somebody else's profile. Get ideas, yes. But you be you.

I once saw that a guy copied my "What are you looking for?" comments verbatim and used them in his. So apparently, we were both looking for the identical kind of relationship, although he never bothered to send me a message and tell me we were perfect for each other.

If you find it hard to express yourself in writing, that's OK. You're going to learn a new skill. First step in personal growth through online dating. Lots of people say they aren't sure how to describe themselves, or that they're new to this and not sure what to say.

In my first attempt at a profile (back in the '90s when pen and paper was a thing), I began by admitting my struggle and started like this, "I have been trying to describe myself but find that, after several hours, I'm surrounded by piles of crumpled paper, having utterly failed." And then I just kept going. My blunt admission of imperfection became part of my profile and I got lots of responses from men saying my profile stood out from the others because it felt more real.

What you choose to say and how you say it tells others

more than you know. Here are some suggested do's and don'ts:

- Don't brag. We know the dating sites tell you to list your accomplishments, but really—going on about your most recent world tour or your double Master's degree in whatever makes you sound full of yourself.

- Men we've talked to say they are tired of reading all about how impossibly fit, active, well-traveled, and full a woman's life is and all she needs is this one perfect guy to fit into what sounds like the teeny tiny slot she has left for a partner. Find a less overwhelming way of saying you're deliriously happy with your life the way it is.

- Women are tired of reading all about how successful a man is or has been in his career. Tell us something more personal.

- Ask friends or family members to say how they would describe you and include some of that.

- Use your sense of humor sparingly. It's too easy to misunderstand someone's humor before you know them.

- Be original: everybody likes to laugh, walk on the beach, and cuddle. Stay away from that shit. Oh, and apparently all women say they love dark chocolate, so now I'm going to have to take that out of my profile. Or at least say something more original about it. Personally, I'm partial to Trader Joe's 72% cacao.

- Try to avoid lists of attributes. While it might be true that you are "playful, ambitious, considerate, trustworthy, genuine, positive, and thoughtful," you just bored the hell out of us because those words don't evoke any kind of picture of you. It works better if you describe ways in which your "playfulness" shows itself. For example, "I love dancing to Motown while I clean the kitchen." (She dances, she cleans, she loves Motown!)

- Especially avoid long lists of negatives, such as, "No liars, don't bother contacting me if you're chained to your grandchildren, not into yappy dogs that go everywhere with you..." Charming. I'll be right over.

- What you have to offer. It's way more captivating to hear how you express love in a relationship than to hear what you expect from someone else. Comments like: "The joy I feel just being with you," or, "I can't wait to be in your presence. I hope we find each other," are a lot more powerful than "You should be romantic, fit, active, witty, intelligent, and make me laugh."

- Specificity makes all the difference! Don't say you like music, tell us you've loved the Rolling Stones since you were fifteen, or talk about the most recent concert you've been to. Instead of saying you like gardening, tell us you proudly harvested your first crop of cherry tomatoes from your back patio. Don't just say you like Netflix, tell us you got hooked on *House of Cards* (which also tells us you're interested in politics). Get the drift?

- Show us your personality. Try to write the same way you speak. How to test for this? Read your profile out loud to yourself. You'll know where it needs tweaking, because it'll sound wrong when you hear it.

- If you generally use slang, put it in your profile. Are you "very close" to your grandchildren or do they "rock your world"?

- Don't say you have a good sense of humor, say something witty or amusing. Or at the very least, look for another word to describe your humor other than "good." I personally like words like "warped," "twisted," and "bent," but that's just me. Or state who your favorite comedian is.

- Spelling and grammar count! Maybe it's a typo, or maybe your fingers are too huge for your keyboard. But honestly, it's a bad look to put something out there that's full of errors. So spell-check your profile before you post it, and find that wonderful friend or family member to proofread it for you.

- If you're really stuck, try to get a friend or someone who loves you to review what you've written. Bottom line, it needs to sound like you and give the reader a sense of who you are.

Want more? The Appendix is filled with ideas to help you write a better profile.

Here are a couple of profiles we made up, to show you what *not* to do:

First off, let me say I love my dog. A lot. I take him everywhere; in fact he sleeps right next to me in my bed. He's in all my pictures. Here are some pics of my dog without me. I'm looking for a woman who is smart, sweet, affectionate, healthy, active, drama-free, no baggage, is comfortable in her own skin—and loves my dog. My main pic online is a blurred selfie with my sunglasses and a baseball cap on, taken from about twenty feet away, at night. My other pic is a morning-hair selfie I took while lying in bed the other morning (with my dog). There's also a photo of me from thirty years ago so you can appreciate how good I used to look. I say I'm 5'9"but I'm really 5'6". I believe an "average" body has about forty extra pounds to it. But my partner should be fit. And sexy.

Or this:

I like romantic walks on the beach, cuddling, and sharing a glass of good wine (I don't drink the cheap stuff). I'm looking for "the one"—you know, the one who will pay for my expensive wine habit and many travel fantasies. You should be at least six feet tall so I can wear heels, and you should be slim, fit, manly yet not a sports freak yet vulnerable, have lots of money, be honest, have impeccable integrity, and be able to make me laugh all the time because I love to laugh.

I am witty and intelligent, fit, healthy and environmentally aware, and you should be too. I've traveled to exotic places that if I mention them, you will think I'm really special. Like Oman. Have you ever been to Oman?

And here's an example of an actual profile written by someone who's also tired of all the bad profiles out there:

"To save time: 5'2"-325 lbs. last visited a gym in '04. Hate humor, prefer depression. Live in mother's basement. Hate travel, prefer watching *NCIS* reruns. Relish pics of your ex, dog, kids, horse, and parents (I want to date them all). I live to eat GMOs, and believe Trump is a secret member of Mensa."

This guy is showing us his humor and personality, along with his values. It's the kind of profile that will get attention, at least from us. If you don't appreciate sarcasm, I guess he wouldn't be for you.

How Long Should a Profile Be?

In general, something around two to four paragraphs is about right. Too long and you sound like you're having a manic episode. Not only that, people tend not to read long profiles unless you are incredibly witty and entertaining, which most of us are not.

Too short—like one or two sentences—and we not only don't get a sense of who you are, you don't seem serious about this and we move on.

Some sites restrict the length of your profile, so you may need to edit it down for those.

How Old are You—Really?

Most of us are in denial about aging, so the temptation to lie about your age can be irresistible. We're tempted to put the age we want to be rather than the age we actually are. No Bueno.

Men we've talked to admit they lie more than women about their age, which surprised us until we ran into this phenomenon quite a bit online. Men who are sixty-five, pretending to be fifty-seven so they can pick up on women in their early fifties—serious fakery. It might get you in the door, but when we find out, we're gone and you've wasted your time.

You blow the whole "honesty" thing if you lie right off the bat. Some people will put a fake age at the top and then reveal their true age in the profile. Guess they're hoping once you see their picture and read about them, their age won't matter as much.

Having reached a milestone birthday I thought made me sound much older, I once took a year off my actual age in a profile (kinda like the psychology of $9.99 vs. $10.00) and felt so guilty that after a day I ran back in and changed it.

It's up to you. But remember, if you lie, you also have to adjust all the dates in your stories when you get talking and eventually you'll have to 'fess up, which is a whole big mess, so our advice is bite the bullet and put that real number in there.

Most people put an age range they're interested in. If you're older than their upper limit, give them a try anyway. Sometimes they'll make an exception. However, your age should be somewhat close to their limit. And if you set an age range for your own profile, be careful of being too restrictive.

And what can we say about people (because apparently women do this, too) who seek partners young enough to be their children's age? We laugh and move on. But seriously, guys, it's no longer as likely that much-younger women will be interested in you (I guess if you have piles of money, you might be able to). But a ten-year difference at this age and you look a little too much like Grandpa.

I don't know about the rest of you, but we are constantly doing the math when we imagine the future with a new partner. The older among us are staring directly into the face of mortality. The end of the road has never felt so real as when you are contemplating starting a new relationship at this time of life. Not to be a total downer, but images of wheelchairs, cancer treatments, and deathbeds cross my mind as I stare at the pics posted on dating sites.

On the bright side, you may have only ten or fifteen years together, so maybe you can view this process as being less of a pressure-filled decision than it was when you were young and trying to pick someone to have babies with and stay with for decades. (That was some of my dark humor. Sorry.)

OK, back to the lighter stuff.

"I'll Take Perfection, Please"

Most sites offer a place for you to describe your "perfect match," but don't go there! It only encourages you to believe that perfection exists. It doesn't. And it emboldens you to make a list of unobtainable attributes that will freak out all of us normal people and we'll never contact you because you sound impossible to please.

Some people have cleverly gotten around this question of the perfect match by saying something like "my ideal date is when I'm already thinking about the second date while we're in the middle of the first," or "my perfect match is when we both feel like we've known each other for years." But don't use those lines, because everybody else already has and you'll sound like a hack.

Geography: How far away is too far?

Let's face it: we'd all like to find someone who lives nearby. One less obstacle to dating and mating. Small-town people are more likely to be open to long-distance dating—but if you live in one, don't expect to get positive responses from people who live in big cities and have all kinds of choices.

One guy I was chatting with online lived in a large city and said he wasn't willing to date anyone unless they lived within five minutes of his place, preferably in his building! He was kidding, but not really. Another guy who lived in a small town said, "There are only about seven women online within fifty miles of me."

So sometimes you have to reach out, but the farther you reach, the more complicated dating gets. There's the driving, the question of where to meet, sleeping arrangements (can you say "awkward"?), and what to do if it works out because for most of us, long-distance romance is a means to an end, not a lifestyle.

If you're willing to move, say so in your profile and you might get more people interested. If you're searching outside your immediate area and relocating is not your idea of fun, ask in your profile if they are willing to move if a relationship develops.

Retired people are generally more flexible about long-distance dating than those who have jobs. All that "gotta work" stuff gets in the way of traveling for a date. But don't assume a retired person will be more flexible about moving. Many of us have already moved to be near those grandchildren we're addicted to, and we're not going anywhere!

Meeting someone out of your area carries a few more safety issues for women, so it's a better idea to suggest that the two of you meet in your town at first.

There's more about long-distance relationships on page 115. For now, we'll say only that life is simpler when you search closer to home.

How Heavy are Those Bags?

"Baggage" is one of the most overused words in the profiles of online dating sites. Which is interesting, since the older we are, the more baggage we tend to have.

What's baggage? It's the trail of life experience, drama, and trauma that follows us through life, clinging to us like a whiny toddler. It includes our history of previous relationships or lack thereof (including the actual ex-spouses and partners), our kids, grandkids, the deaths we've experienced, the emotional pain we've gone through, the break-ups, health issues, and financial situations, to name a few. Basically, all the stuff that has made you who you are today, and by the time you get to this age, it's quite a pile. Many of us are pretty banged up, in one way or another.

Some people proudly state in their profiles that they have "no baggage." Wait a minute. The only people without baggage were born, like, five minutes ago and they still experienced birth trauma, right? What they probably mean is they believe they've cleaned up their messes. Still. Nobody is a blank slate, perfectly free of any issues, physical or mental or emotional. That's ridiculous.

The real issue is how much of your baggage is attached to you at the moment, and how much room you have for somebody else's. Are they (or you) going through a divorce or emotionally suffering from a break-up or death? Constantly on-call for babysitting the grandchildren? Got kids at home? Do you have financial problems or lots of debt? Taking care of an elderly parent? Is your ex hanging around creating problems in your life? Do you or they have health problems, either mental or physical?

If they can't handle yours or you can't handle theirs, it's time to move along. But it's usually not that simple, because baggage is everywhere: under our seat, in our overhead compartment, and stored way below in that place where it's cold and dark and we don't like to talk about. This means that sometimes we don't realize how heavy the baggage is until we've handed our hearts over.

It's easier to end a connection before strong feelings develop. It's quite another to have to do it later down the road, if baggage starts getting in the way.

Examples:

You're really active, and that bad knee/hip/back of hers flares up so she can't do much anymore.

He said his job wasn't very demanding and he had time for a relationship, but starts traveling extensively and is exhausted whenever he's home.

You both started out enjoying a simple, laid-back lifestyle but her hard-drinking son loses his job and is sleeping on Mom's couch again.

Ugh. Can't we just run through a meadow together, hand in hand, into the sunset?

No. I mean, sure, some of you have your health, the kids are grown and successfully launched, your investments are paying off, you're now retired and life is good. Maybe all you have are some war wounds from your divorce or the death of your spouse, and that's great. But don't expect it to be that way for most people you meet.

At this age, many of us are at max baggage, and it's strapped to our backs, weighing down our shoulders and straining our arms. Some of the zippers are broken, with sweaters and shoes spilling out the sides.

Accept it or don't but know that the bag check will be part of the bargain as we stumble through that meadow looking for love again. Deciding if we are prepared to take on another person's baggage at this age takes a balance of compassion along with a realistic evaluation of what we are willing and able to handle.

Let's Talk about Drama—Everyone Else Is

Along with "no baggage," "no drama" is the next most over-used phrase in online profiles, leading many of us to ask, "Wait, is drama the same thing as baggage or does baggage lead to drama or is drama contained within baggage?" This is where jargon will get you.

There's a lot to unpack about the possible meaning of "no drama." Some people may be reeling from the ending of their last tumultuous relationship and remembering how crappy the relationship death throes felt.

For others, it may mean they're looking for someone who

isn't high maintenance, demanding, high strung, or possessive. Or they're hoping you don't freak out if they're five minutes late to dinner.

There *are* some people who feed off of crises. Their lives aren't complete unless they're constantly embroiled in highly emotional situations. By the same token, there are people who have a low threshold for handling any of life's problems. These two people should not get together.

However, some people don't realize they keep unconsciously picking the same kind of partner, repeating old patterns and ending up in "drama" situations, over and over. In that case, do not pass "Go," do not collect $200. Go back to self-reflection until you learn how not to pick high-drama partners.

Another possibility, upon deeper reflection, is that the person trying to avoid drama is actually creating their own but blaming it on their partner. Always late? Flirt with others at parties? Closed off emotionally? It's all about you? Expect people to dish you up some drama.

Usernames

Of the several parts of your online existence, this one matters least, yet it's one you might find yourself agonizing over for hours. I know I did. You can use your first name, but it'll likely be taken, so using your name with some numbers usually works.

The dating site may suggest a name for you—usually something like FUN before your name, as in FunRalphie. Yuck. They may also suggest using HOT in front of your name. HotRalphie is possibly worse than FunRalphie. In general, don't lead with how sexy or hot or amazing you are, like: Hot Guy, Superman, Loverboy, Lovemachine. Gak.

One person who was likely sick of the whole exercise selected "Username4usernames," which we kinda liked. Keep it simple.

Here We Go!

> "We're all hoping to find that person
> who will simply love us for the
> awesome fucking disaster we are."
>
> —Author Unknown

Starting the Search

YOU'VE PICKED A dating site, and you've entered your info, so it's time to settle in with your laptop or your phone, a nice cup of tea or a glass of wine, and start looking at profiles. Actually, tea is way too polite of a drink for searching online for the next/last love of your life. Go with alcohol.

No matter which site you're on, the first thing you'll see is the main photo of the person you're selecting. Some sites will have a neat little box next to the pic with basic info like age, location, marital status—and we wish there was a little space to indicate if they're jerks and everyone who's ever dated them hates them now, but there isn't. Anyway, the main pic is the first of the first impressions.

You'll see people who look way too old to be the age they claim to be (aka "hopeful liars in denial" or extreme sun exposure). You'll see people who are your age but remind you of your dead grandparents and scare the shit out of you: *Do I look that old, too, but don't realize it?* There will be all the blurred and "Back when I was young and hot" and "Guess which one I am in this group?" photos we warned you about earlier. There will also be headless pics, pics with spouses (we hope they're exes, but still. Really, people?) and scowling faces staring out from La-Z-Boy recliners.

Or this one, which gets the award for "What was he thinking?" A photo of Einstein, followed by a photo of daffodils in bloom, followed by a photo of an old pioneer wagon and finally—wait for it—a guy with no shirt sitting on a bed with his back to the camera, hunched over a laptop.

Once you find some halfway-decent pics of people who look like they might be interesting, you start reading profiles, looking for someone who sounds normal or abnormal in the same way you are normal or abnormal.

I personally like the sites that outline some of the most important issues of lifestyle and values, before you have to read the profile. Things like: Marital status? Do they smoke? Pets? Religion? Politics? Drink alcohol? Body type (although wishful thinking is a huge part of this one, so…grain of salt). These categories are full of deal-breakers; knowing this upfront can save you from having to meet up with a politically repulsive, not-quite-divorced chain-smoker. Unless you're into that.

During the search, you'll (hopefully) receive messages from people interested in you, although if your experience is anything like ours, 99% of those are, well, to be polite, off the Richter scale of what you're looking for. But occasionally you'll get a message from Mr. or Ms. 1%; someone who looks interesting to you, sounds interesting in their profile, and doesn't have any of your deal-breakers. So you write them back.

If you are new to online dating, the dance leading up to a first date looks something like this: look at pics, get discouraged, search profiles, get tired of searching, finally find someone who interests you and then send a message to them, never hear back from them, look at more profiles, get sick of reading about people who love to laugh and cuddle while watching Netflix, sift through people who are too tall, too short, too old, too far away, too young, too religious, or not religious enough, and then occasionally find one who both looks and sounds like a person you might enjoy meeting—and who actually answers you when you message them. Then comes texting, phone calls, and eventually, maybe, an actual 3-D date with a human.

Don't stop when you find your first connection. Keep searching. Keep messaging. Keep responding. That fabulous-sounding person who wrote back to you and suggested that the two of you meet will confuse the hell out of you when they suddenly disappear.

If you do actually get to a date, be prepared that most first dates are "one and done," because of that phenomenon called "chemistry." Or worse, they're one and done due to "Whoa, do you ever not look like your photos."

On the other hand, if you're not finding anybody out there you could possibly imagine dating or you're not getting responses to your messages, try expanding your search for age, distance, and anything else you can stand to compromise on.

Be prepared for all these steps to be scary and challenging.

When I first went online, I was happily searching away, reading profiles and occasionally messaging back and forth with men who caught my interest. It was great fun. I didn't panic until the moment a guy asked if he could call me, and then I came unglued. I tried to put him off. I tried to make my panic funny by admitting I had never done this before and I was afraid. Of what, I had no idea. Afraid of a phone call?

Eventually, he messaged me off the ledge and we had a very stilted, very uncomfortable (at least for me) phone conversation. I alternately paced around the room and flopped down on the couch. I was a mess. The silences were excruciating, the laughter self-conscious and stilted, and I couldn't wait to hang up.

This is how rusty you can get after being in a long-term relationship, and I consider myself a reasonably confident, outgoing, social person. So I was shocked to find myself getting this tangled up about a simple phone call. But I'd done it. I'd broken through the first barrier. And I will always be thankful to that guy, whoever he was. (Never did meet him.)

The Art of Messaging

We're now at the first "live action" portion of the dance. Past the pics, past the pre-written blah blah blah. Time for "Hey," "Hi," "What up?" or hopefully other, more intelligent-sounding chit-chat.

Make your initial message brief but answer-worthy. "Great profile" is lame, and "You sound wonderful. Wanna get married?" is a tad too fast—although after a while of browsing through dozens of photos and profiles, you may be exhausted enough to throw any old thing out there. If so, put the phone/laptop/iPad down for a while, and go take a nap.

When you're ready again, reread their profile and comment on something you both have in common, or something they wrote that you found interesting. When you send someone a message, they'll also get your pic and profile.

Put a question in your message, so they have something to respond to. But not any old question. A guy once wrote me a message that said, "Hey, love your smile. Will you have dinner with me at (local restaurant) tonight? Here's my phone number." Um, no.

Oh and avoid sending those non-verbal "winks," "nudges," and "favorites"; everybody hates them. However, it's worth noting that some sites choose pics for you and ask you to decide if you're interested or not, or to choose between two possible candidates. If you click on their profile or say you're interested, the person will receive a "like" or something similar from you without your meaning to. Very clever, these sites.

And just like the fact that you won't respond to 99% of people who write to you, there are as many who won't respond to your messages. When I first joined, I wrote super-thoughtful and sincere messages to guys who never responded. I took it personally at first. Don't. We've read long lectures online from people saying it's rude not to answer people who write to you. Up to you. We think it's fair not to answer every little "hi" that comes across your screen.

Some people aren't online anymore, but the site keeps profiles up unless you find the right button way inside the bowels of the website that allows you to hide or erase it. And if a person is actively online, keep in mind that you're not the only one writing to them, or they may be dating someone at the moment and not checking the site, or whatever. I've heard from several guys a few days or weeks after my initial message, when their dance card finally had some space.

Anyway, so let's say you now have a messaging relationship with a person you've met through the dating site. Everybody has their own preferences about how much messaging they do before the first phone call and deciding whether to meet. Some write for a while and others prefer to do a face-to-face more quickly.

Another note here: if you write to someone and they don't respond, do not keep bugging them. One guy messaged me when I wasn't signed up anymore, but when I renewed he was like an eager puppy: "Wow, I found you! I saw your profile a few months ago and wrote to you, but then it went away but now you're back!" He said this like we were best buddies from high school and we lost contact only because he'd lost my number.

Then he wrote another whole long message about how thrilled he was that I was back, and how much we had in common, and that we'd get along great. I didn't answer. Needless to say, I didn't find his pics or his profile appealing. He wrote again, and then found me on another site and wrote once more, until I felt like I was being cyber-stalked and finally asked him to please stop.

Then he got all mad and hurt, like we were having our first fight. I wrote back and apologized for snapping at him, but at least I never heard from him again. Does that make me a bad person? Maybe. As the message-sender, you should take the hint if someone ignores you.

The First Phone Call

The phone call is the second stage of the "interview," and with it comes a whole new level of fun and anxiety. Hearing their voice, your voice, demonstrating an ability to carry on a coherent and hopefully witty conversation with a complete stranger in an exercise designed to mutually impress one another—life doesn't get any simpler, does it?

Not to scare you any more than we already have, but I had a date with one guy in his sixties who told me he wouldn't go out with any woman whose voice sounded like an "old lady" on the phone. Wow. I guess the message is that we all secretly know we're getting old, but be careful not to look it or sound it, 'cuz out here in dating world, we're expected to fake eternal youth.

We've heard stories where people skipped the phone call and when they met, the person's voice grated on them so badly there was no way they could imagine a relationship. Is there any advice here? No, except to say a phone conversation before meeting is a good idea, and that there is no end to the levels on which people judge and are judged. Still, we persist.

So back to the phone call. Once you have a phone number, check to make sure it's the right one by texting first and then arranging a time to talk. Don't surprise the person with a call that may catch them with an armload of groceries or worse, on another date.

Whether to use face-time is up to you. (Depending on what level of techno-dinosaur you are, you may not even know what face-time is. It's this button on your phone that allows you to see a person you're on the phone with.) And if you use it, you'll get more information about each other's personality, but you know, the whole staring at each other thing while trying to think of what to say while trying to hold the phone at the right angle so your face doesn't look weird… It's like a first date, but worse. I'm into the old-fashioned audio call, at least initially, while Debi (younger generation) does it high-tech style without missing a beat.

The first call is an opportunity to share an overview of each other's history: where you're from, a little about your family, your lifestyle, your work. Stay away from those stories about how your ex lied about you and now you're alienated from your kids, or how the damn cable company said they'd be there between nine and twelve and they haven't shown up (which pisses you off to no end), and your cat just brought in another dead mouse. Keep it light. There's not enough context yet in your connection for them to understand that you're actually quite a delightful person and not a scattered, bitter weirdo.

As a screening tool, a phone call can save you from a painful date. I had been messaging one guy, and things were going well—then we had the call. Twenty minutes into it, I was holding the phone out from my ear while he continued babbling about this guy he met at a convention in Ohio, which led to being offered a position with blah blah blah, before which he'd been monologuing the details of his avocado harvest. Did he ask any questions to find out about me? None. I saw the movie of our date in my mind's eye, with me fake-smiling and nodding my head at appropriate moments while trying to stay awake.

The funny (not funny) thing about it is he said he really enjoyed our conversation and suggested we meet. I couldn't find a polite way to say, "Thank you but I'm full up on factoids about avocados," so I lied. Yes I did. I lied and told him I was going out of town that week and then luckily for me, he was going out of town the next week so I was able to slither away with some generic "met somebody else" excuse when he finally got back in touch.

I still haven't figured out how to tell someone that, now that we've talked, a date will not be necessary. It's like failing the phone conversation portion of the interview, and who wants to tell someone *that* news? So we go on, with the little white lies and the weenie moves designed to protect the feelings of near-strangers.

A final note: Some women are nervous about giving out their cell phone number, but the way we look at it, they don't know where you live and if they become a pain, you can always block their number. Personally, neither of us have experienced a problem resulting from giving out phone numbers. Best not to give landline numbers out, since your address can be traced.

Texting

Once you've had the phone call, the texting exchange often starts, which is its own little world. Texting with its immediacy and cartoon emojis, can be great fun. Texting can create what we like to call "banter," and banter can lead immediately to chemistry because it usually means you are starting to "get" each other.

But if you already use texting (and hopefully you do,

because there is skill involved, as well as danger), you know it can lead to incredible amounts of misunderstanding because we think we get each other and we're texting and we or they say something that's taken the wrong way, and then you're stuck in mop-up operations or maybe blow the whole thing. So limit the amount of texting until you know the person better.

Not only that, but people tend to fire off texts without much proofreading and can end up sending messages they wish they hadn't. One guy I hadn't met yet accidentally sent me a "kiss" emoji that apparently was next to his "thumbs up" emoji.

A word to those who should be wearing their glasses when they text: Autocorrect is *not* your friend. Debi admits she's notorious for shooting off a text without her glasses on and then having to apologize for looking like a two-year-old playing with her parents' phone. Oh, and make sure that you're sending your text to the right person. Nothing like sending a gushy, romantic text to the person you just broke up with.

There's another thing with any form of writing—be it messaging on the dating site, emailing, or texting—and that's realizing you've been writing and writing and writing to someone but nobody is making plans to meet up. It's another one of those things where women tend to wait for the guy to ask them out, and the guy isn't doing it but says he's interested in her. Confusing, right? My daughter says this happens in all age groups, not only with older people, and a friend of hers came up with the concept of "textationships" to describe the phenomenon.

And remember that what used to be known as "drunk dialing" has become "drunk texting." Usually occurs when you've had a few and you get this urgency to share all the fun you're having, but ends up with texts full of out-of-focus selfies and embarrassing sentiments containing way too many exclamation points.

Or, after you've broken up with someone you were dating, and you're not meeting anybody interesting and feeling sappy and nostalgic and then forget why you broke up in the first place and decide to zing them with a friendly little text message. Whatever the reason, you will come to regret drunk texting, so keep the damn phone in your pocket.

How Much Talking Before Meeting

In cyber-time, a week is like several light-years. If someone says they're busy or out of town but, "Hey let's get together at the end of the month," chances are it's not going to happen—either because they're lying and it's an easy way to fade out, or one or both of you won't remember each other when the time comes. People move fast in online dating. So many faces, so little time.

Similarly, if you don't keep the communication going, people move on, assuming you're not interested enough. Check the site or sites you're on, daily if possible, and keep the ball rolling by responding to messages.

As previously mentioned, some people like to meet right away; others prefer to message and/or talk for a while before going the extra (and more stressful) step of meeting. Personally, we like to find out a little bit about a person before we run right out there and put ourselves through the anxiety of a first date.

A Little Note about Scammers

We're going to brush lightly over this and advise you to look to the dating sites and other places for information about how to avoid scammers and "catfishers," because this is a serious issue, and not one we feel qualified to give advice about, except for some hints about what to watch out for.

Scammers are often looking for money, or someone to take care of them. They may try to become your "perfect" person and hopefully get you to fall in love with them before they ask for cash, while others get right to it and ask you to "lend" them some money—not because they don't have any, but because, you see... (insert elaborate story of being ripped off or not getting paid yet, or someone stole their identity and screwed up their credit score or they lost their credit card or left their wallet at home but they'll definitely pay you right back, how embarrassing to have to ask, blah blah blah).

All we will say is never ever send or give money to somebody you meet online. Probably not even after you marry them (kidding).

Catfishers are people who pose as someone other than who they are; sometimes because they don't believe anyone will like them if you were to actually meet, sometimes because they are married, and sometimes because they are sick people who live in a fantasy world.

I got temporarily deceived by someone online once. He (or whoever it was) "liked" or "favorited" me, so I checked him out. His photo was gorgeous—should've been a red flag, but I preferred to believe he was interested in me. Heart palpitating, I wrote to him, and he wrote back, saying very complimentary things about me and my photos and profile. He said I seemed to be a "very special kind of woman," and it would be "an honor" to get to know me. I couldn't believe it, but I wanted to, so I did. We wrote back and forth that evening. His writing style was a little more formal than I was used to, but no biggie.

He gave me his email address and asked for my contact info. I gave him my cell phone number. The phrase "too good to be true" echoed in my brain as I fell asleep that night. Nevertheless, I was hopeful. He wrote again the next morning through private email. I was somewhat surprised he didn't call or text me after getting my number.

The list of things he mentioned being proficient in started to sound a little unrealistic. Trail runner, biker, hiker, tennis player, golfer, skier, snowboarder, soccer player, and also accomplished on guitar and keyboards and went to the gym three or four times a week. Oh, come on.

His email address revealed his last name, so I Googled him. He'd told me where he grew up and I knew what town he lived in now (he was about 150 miles away from where I lived). I found a professional bio of him on LinkedIn that matched his name, town, and indicated where he'd been educated, which matched up with what he'd told me, except for one thing. The photo of the guy on LinkedIn wasn't the same guy as the photo on the dating site.

I downloaded the LinkedIn photo and compared it to his dating site photo, trying to imagine them as the same guy. I thought maybe he'd put a much younger self on the dating site. The nose was somewhat similar, as was the chin, but hmmmm…. What was going on? I went back to find his profile online. Suddenly, it was "no longer available." Red flags were flying everywhere.

That evening, when he emailed me yet again, the formality and oddness of his language seemed even more extreme. Plus, he spent an unusual amount of time describing the kind of food he liked. The line that finally took it over the edge was "I like Idaho potato." It was time to call this guy's bluff. Of course I could have simply ignored his messages and moved on, but sometimes, curiosity gets the best of me.

It was time for a consultation with Debi. After we finished cry-laughing about "Idaho potato," we strategized how to handle him. I sent him a message, "Hey, this emailing is fun and all, but how about we chat on the phone next?" I suggested he give me his number and I'd call him the next day, or he could call me. I never heard from him again, and I guess I'll never know what he was up to. He never asked for money or anything else. Practicing his English? Living in his mother's basement, playing out fantasies? Mysteries of the universe.

Want to limit your exposure to some types of questionable people online? Watch out for these warning signs:

- No photos, or amazingly good-looking photos they may have "borrowed" from online. There is a way to "reverse image" a photo, so you can find out if someone downloaded a photo from somewhere online. Google this to get instructions.

- An unwillingness to meet or being willing to meet only in places other than their home

- Stories about themselves that either don't add up, or sound too good to be true

- Ridiculously younger than you, but asks to go out with you

So Many Choices—or Not

If you're lucky, your dance card will fill up like TV's *Bachelor* or *Bachelorette*. So many people interested in you. Every morning is like Christmas—checking messages to see how many people love you today. Even if you don't hit the mother lode, you may find yourself talking to several people at once, and eventually dating more than one person. We call this "multi-dating," and it can be quite overwhelming if you are used to dating one person at a time, which most of us are or were in the natural world before the Internet.

I don't mean to be cheeky, but I once got so confused that I started a chart of guys I was messaging with. Name, age, key word to remind me who he was. And I'm talking about only four or five people here. My goal was to get to one person as quickly as possible, but not to narrow my choices too soon.

You have to be sensitive about how you manage multiple prospects. We heard about one guy who lined up several dates in a row in the same coffee bar, one after the other. Kind of a speed-dating experiment. It all went well until the women started realizing what was going on and he lost them all. More on dating multiple people on page 80.

You'll likely get some responses if you reach out to enough people. The trick here is to be realistic. You may be surprised to find out your expectations are too high.

Yes, but What if Nobody Likes Me?

It's a fact. Sometimes no one you like seems interested in you, and it feels like crap.

- First, check for the obvious. Women's profiles often come up in our own searches (and they appear to be hetero women looking for hetero men). They must've checked the wrong box when asked if they were a "woman looking for a man" or a "man looking for a woman," or a "woman looking for a woman," or a "man looking for a man." I guess those might seem like confusing choices. But if you get that wrong, you really should stay away from cyberspace. And toaster-ovens.

- Change it up. Rewrite your profile. Swap out your main photo. Take some new photos.

- Join a different dating site. Some sites don't have enough members, or members of your demographic. I tried a site that Debi had great success with but was a big bust for me. Zero. Zip. Nada.

Except for that one guy who responded with "Hey Baby, here's my number. Call me." I didn't.

- Check your expectations. Are you writing to people who are outside of what's realistic for you? Are you ignoring messages from people whose looks you don't find appealing? Maybe it's time to get past the photos and read some profiles instead. You might find a gem in there who simply doesn't look like you hoped they would, but could end up being a great match.

- And here's a really radical idea: If there aren't enough available people where you are, consider moving. I live in a small town and I absolutely love it here, but it's slim pickins and long-distance relationships suck, so it's an idea.

Here's a story to illustrate this last point. Back in the early days of the Internet, when I was a single mother in my late forties and tried online dating for the first time, it was very basic. All you could do was write something about yourself, title it, and wait for responses. No photos could be uploaded and there were no search parameters; your post could be viewed all over the world.

A guy answered my post who lived almost 400 miles away, had a dog, was a vegetarian, and didn't drink alcohol. I was looking for a local, non-pet-owning meat-eater who enjoyed a cocktail now and then. But his messages were interesting and fun and deep in ways that really appealed to me. Our connection quickly became very strong.

Over the weeks that followed, we asked each other all the important questions about relationships, our histories, values, what we believed in, our insecurities, our hopes for the future—everything. And we cyber-flirted like mad.

By the time we met, three months later, feelings of love had already blossomed. If he'd been able to post a photo, I would likely have overlooked him. We did planes, trains, automobiles, and long-distance phone calls in order to spend weekends together. We fell crazy in love.

Six months later, he moved in with me and we married nine months afterward. The dog came, too, and I learned to eat more fish. We were together for eighteen years. Which goes to show you that sometimes the things you think are deal-breakers turn out not to be deal-breakers.

Now You See 'Em, Now You Don't

The term "ghosting" refers to a common phenomenon in online dating. Actually, it should be called "the vanishing act" because that's what it is (although you might continue to be haunted by images of the person floating around online).

Be prepared at all phases of a relationship to be "ghosted," but especially before you actually meet in person. You may have been bantering back and forth and looking forward to their next message... which never comes.

There are a zillion reasons people suddenly disappear. It could be they've met someone they like, or they were interested in you but then they weren't, their cat died or their attention span was diverted to some shiny thing over in the corner. Some people will tell you why they're no longer interested; most won't. Don't sweat it.

There was one guy I was writing to who seemed fun and interesting at first, but eventually his messages devolved into a constant stream of sexual innuendo, and I lost interest. Rather than ghosting him, I wrote back and told him it sounded to me like he was only interested in sex, and it wasn't what I was looking for. I never heard from him again. (He was probably too busy having sex.)

Dry Spells

Even if you felt like the Bachelor/Bachelorette at first, with a deluge of people interested in you, don't get cocky, because it doesn't last forever. If you go tip-toeing through the tulips, dating and rejecting because you're sure the perfect partner is going to show up any day now, you will eventually hit a dry spell where the deluge winds down to a trickle or a drought. We're telling you this so that you know the supply isn't endless and so you don't accidentally pass on a really good connection because you got drunk on the fire hose of possibilities.

Or, maybe you've been very careful and deliberate, taking your time, and you met somebody and started an actual 3-D relationship. But then it didn't work out and you went back on the site assuming it was going to be like when you first went on and there were lots of choices, only to find the same faces staring back at you that you didn't like the first time, along with a paltry few new faces that once again remind you of your grandparents. Don't panic.

Maybe give the search a rest for a while. Take your profile down for a bit (so you don't become one of those faces everybody gets tired of) and go find something else to do. You also might try another site, but just sayin'—dry spells happen. A month later, there's likely to be a completely new landscape.

Virtual Chemistry

Let's be frank: "chemistry" is the socially acceptable way of making lust sound like a science project. We all get what's being talked about, but this way, it sounds like a mysterious process involving beakers in a lab instead of sweat and bodily fluids, and nobody has to blush when you talk about it at cocktail parties.

Virtual chemistry, then, is sexual attraction via messaging/

texting/phone calls before you meet in person. It can happen in that back-and-forth banter, as you develop a sense of familiarity or "getting" each other, when there's an ease to conversation, the ability to make each other laugh, and little flirtations. This, however, can lead to sexting (the sexual version of texting) and phone sex and all kinds of getting ahead of yourselves, so watch out (unless that kind of thing floats your boat, in which case, enjoy!).

Virtual chemistry is a great indicator that you two will have actual chemistry when you meet in person, but not always. I once developed a lovely chemistry with a guy during our messaging phase; we had lots in common, a similar way of communicating, and developed some good-natured teasing and flirting via text. I thought we'd really hit it off, but when we met, the energy felt friendly but did not lead to the exchange of any bodily fluids.

Much more on chemistry later.

Don't Let Those Red Flags Smack You in the Face

A red flag is like that smarter, wiser voice inside your head that starts to lecture you when you're about to wander down a dark alley. It usually sounds just like your mother when she used to stop you on your way out the door with, "Hey, where do you think you're going?"

In dating, red flags are indications you and the man or woman you met online might not be a match; tendencies, qualities, values, or a lifestyle a person displays that aren't for you. You might get whiffs of red flags in someone's online persona (*Hmmm, she has a pet tarantula,* or *Wow, look at that photo of him with his gun collection*).

Each red flag may not mean it's a "no," but they are minuses in that big scoreboard of "Should I or shouldn't I?" Red flags are like mental notes to find out more. And maybe this is a good place to talk about being "set in our ways." Being on our own for a while plus whatever that thing is that makes people more rigid with age can become a factor when we're considering a new potential partner.

So be careful of creating a big fat list of red flags and deal-breakers that end up excluding almost everybody as potential partners. I recently talked to a woman in her late sixties who was considering going online to find a mate but then she rattled off her list: he had to be fit and active, have no health problems, eat organic food, own a nice home, and have enough money to travel the world with her. I had to break it to her that, if that guy existed in her age range, he was likely on the hunt for forty-somethings.

If you have a lot of conditions and can't or won't pare down your list of red flags and deal-breakers, you may be better off living alone and getting a dog. But dogs tend to chew furniture and pee on the rug, so…yeah.

Red flag story: One guy with a "no photo" profile (red flag) approached me online. He said the reason he had no pictures was because he was separated (flag) and didn't want his ex to find out he was online so the divorce would go smoothly (flag). He gave me his work email and said he would write me from there because he was still living in the same house as his ex and she read his emails (flag).

I was somewhat sympathetic because there was a period when I was divorcing that my ex and I had to share a home for economic reasons. This man from the dating site sounded distraught and in need of someone to talk to. He asked to get together for a walk, as friends.

My inner-mother voice started yelling at me, so I said, "Not while you're still living in the same house with your ex." He said he understood but would like to keep writing to me. He needed a friend, so I agreed. (See how easily you can get into trouble?)

He continued to write from time to time, often complaining about how unreasonable his ex was being about the divorce. We commiserated about the divorce experience. Then one day, out of the blue, I got an email from a woman who identified herself as this guy's wife. She sent me, by text, pictures of recent emails he'd sent to her, in which he was asking for another chance. The emails were current.

She'd found/snooped (who knows?) all the emails he and I had sent to one another. She thanked me for my ethical stance of refusing to see him but thought she should tell me what was really going on. I apologized to her, and she was very gracious. I never heard from that guy again.

Dating 101 – A Refresher Course

*Beware of those butterflies
you feel when you like someone. It's just
good judgment leaving your body.*

—Author Unknown

Why Am I So Nervous?

*I*F YOU'VE BEEN in a relationship for years, your dating freshness label is way past its due date. "Rusty" doesn't begin to describe it. How to approach the opposite sex? How to ask for a date? How to flirt? What are the rules? *Where* are the rules?

There's this eighteen-year-old inside all of us who went

dormant while we were married because our lives were such a snooze fest, but when you start dating again, this wanton adolescent jumps up and takes over your personality. *Let's get this party started!*

Men go all awkward and horny, and women get nervous and giddy (women get horny too, but like when we were younger, we're not sure if we're allowed). So although we head out there with the belief that we're mature adults who know how to do this life thing, without warning our hormones start raging again (what hormones, right?), we forget how we're supposed to behave, and our adult children start looking at us funny.

The First Date

We arrive at the first date with that idealized collection of their pics in our head, scanning the room for someone who resembles them. There's a good joke going around online:

"If you don't look like your photos when we meet, you're buying me drinks until you do."

—Author Unknown

It usually takes a few seconds for that static, 2-D version of who you thought you were going to meet to mesh with the flesh-and-blood version who walks through the door. Sometimes it's a pleasant surprise, other times the person is shorter, heavier or much older than you were expecting, and you're stuck trying to smile brightly and pretend you're not shocked. Or, God forbid, someone is giving you that disappointed, "Oh, *you're* my date" look. Many a first date has already ended mentally before you sit down. And all because you or they aren't what you appeared to be online.

Debi's first scheduled online date didn't even happen because of the guy's misrepresentation online. She'd had a good online connection with him, but as she walked up to meet him (he hadn't noticed her yet), she got a good look and bolted. Yup. Ran away, back to her car and home. She did call the guy later and gave a polite excuse about why she hadn't shown up. But the situation was so traumatizing that she decided she was done with online dating, closing down her profile and never doing it again. Her kids listened patiently but pushed her to keep going and not get discouraged. She reluctantly set up a date with a different man, and it went much better.

First date safety tip: Meet your date at the venue; don't have them pick you up at your home and don't go to their home. We also suggest that women find out their date's last name before meeting. And then Google the shit out of them. Facebook them. LinkedIn them. It's another way to be more sure they are who they say they are, and that they're not wanted in all fifty states.

Where to Meet

If you're the asker, you get to suggest the venue because you're paying. But you knew that, right?

Meeting for a walk is free but it's not the best option. First of all, you sound cheap. Besides, when you walk, you're side-by-side and don't get to look at each other much, without which you might miss out on the whole chemistry deal—the number one thing people are in search of on a first date. Not only that, a walk could end up being somewhere with no other people, which goes back to safety issues..

One guy noticed from my profile that I liked hiking and so did he. So he asked me if I'd like to go on a hike with him for a first date. Point one? When I hike I'm wearing sports clothing—not particularly fetching for a first impression date. And point two: typically one person walks in front of the other, so there's minimal contact. Worse than a walk. Point three? Remote... again, safety issues. I was pretty sure he was safe, but I gave him my standard line: "I don't go to remote places on a first date. I haven't determined yet if you're an axe murderer." He laughed and got it. We met in a restaurant, had great conversation, joked about axe murderers, and went for a hike on our second date.

Not that murder is a funny topic. We hate having to acknowledge that women actually have to take this into consideration, each and every time. But we do. And guys may need to be reminded of this when they suggest picking you up at your home or taking you to theirs, or hiking, or meeting them somewhere remote. The possible risks are many and they can sneak up on you, disguised as great ideas.

For example, Debi was asked out on a sailing date, which sounded very exciting and romantic, until we remembered it meant she'd be out at sea with a stranger and no cell service.

Going for coffee is cheap and quick, so if you have inklings that the date isn't going to be that great, or as the guy, if your wallet is empty from too many first dates, meeting for coffee might be a good idea. One guy did say in his profile, though, that he never did coffee dates because he thought people acted more like they were at an interview. Maybe it's the caffeine and all that clear-headedness. He preferred dates that included a glass of wine, which generally led to letting one's hair down and being more real. We have to agree, unless of course you don't drink alcohol. Then you won't be dating this guy. Or either of us, most likely.

Next up the scale both in terms of time and money spent is meeting for a drink or drink and appetizers, and beyond that are meals: breakfast, lunch, dinner, or an event. There are lots of clever ideas for where to have first dates, but is a trip to the science museum or ziplining going to set the mood you're looking to create? (I like to avoid any activity that will give me helmet-hair.)

As the asker, suggest a category, as in "Would you like to meet for dinner/coffee/a drink somewhere?" and suggest a few places or ask her where she likes to go. Be careful here, though. If you leave it too open-ended and she picks that super-expensive restaurant on the hill with a view of the city—now what are you going to do?

One guy left it totally up to me with no clues about what he was prepared to shell out for. I had no idea whether he meant coffee, a walk, or dinner. I was tempted to pick the super-expensive restaurant on the hill with a view of the city, but took pity on him, suggested a couple of choices in different categories and price ranges, and told him any of those were fine with me. In the end, he chose, which felt much more comfortable for me.

If you're not a particularly good conversationalist or you're a bit shy, you could pick an activity where there's something to do besides stare at each other and try to think of what to say. Maybe something like a wine-tasting or visiting a museum. But make it something that encourages interaction.

What to Wear

We're going to assume you didn't get to this age without knowing the basics about dressing yourself, so we'll skip the usual "make sure the fabric isn't straining at the seams, wear something you're comfortable in, and check for stains in a brightly lit room" advice.

The temptation at our age might be to try to dress "young and trendy," and while we assume you're leaving behind the old sweater with the elbow patches, it's probably not a good idea to throw on those hip yellow sneakers or the strategically ripped jeans, either. (Although Debi recently had a date with an LA guy, and she went right for those currently-stylish ripped jeans, so maybe it's just us over-sixty people who should stay away from them.)

In general, stick to whatever style you usually wear and feel comfortable in—but the cleaned-up version.

Men, God love 'em, say they'd like their date to be dressed somewhat "sexy." After the age of sixty, however, we women don't exactly rock a cute little sundress anymore, but we recommend women pause before reaching for that super-comfy loose shirt that hides all your bulges but makes you look like a bag lady.

And men, you will impress us if you lose the saggy jeans and tired old T-shirt (or maybe that's just a Southern California uniform). If you want women to look good, let's have a little effort from you, too. A button-down shirt or maybe a T-shirt with a jacket (depending on where we're going) is a nice touch.

Cologne, after-shave, and perfume: Not right away. Your date could be allergic. And scent is one of those things that can turn people off if it's too overwhelming. Once you get to know someone better, you can ask their opinion and go from there.

Hats and sunglasses. Get rid of them at some point during the date. If you're bald, you might as well get it over with, plus we have to be able to check behind the sunglasses for any "crazy" in those eyes.

Take a Breath

You'll be nervous, especially at first. Take a *deep* breath. It gets easier with time. Sorta.

And while we're on the issue of the breath, some great news! There is no longer any reason to worry about bad breath. This is one time we will mention a product, because it ends all that paranoia about whether your breath smells good, and eliminates the need for gum, mints, and all that other crap. It's called SmartMouth. It's in drugstores, it's much more expensive than your usual mouthwash but it works for up to twenty-four hours. Tried and tested.

You're welcome.

The first time I went on an actual, official date after my divorce, I started by freaking out about what to wear. We were meeting at a romantic little Italian place for dinner, so I was going for kinda dressed up but casual but not looking like I was trying too hard. Do guys go through this? I bet you don't.

After most of my closet had been emptied onto my bed, I finally found a comfortable dress I thought might hit the right note. Shoes, shoes. No, not heels. No, not flats. I needed sandals, but not any sandals I had. Dashed to the store and found some slightly dressed-up yet casual but not-trying-too-hard sandals.

I drove down the road and as I got closer to the restaurant, my armpits started dripping and my heart started pounding. I'd had several phone conversations with my date already and many texts, but suddenly I couldn't imagine what we'd talk about. I was tempted to make a quick U-turn, go back home, and crawl under the covers. Instead, I called my daughter, who was in her thirties. Told her I was hyperventilating. Know what she said to me?

"Mom, chill. It's going to be fine. It's just a person, and you're having dinner and talking. Maybe it'll turn into something, maybe it won't. Don't stress it." My daughter is brilliant that way. She knows me well, and is much cooler than I am.

By the time I hung up, I was all zenned out and ready for my date. I cruised into the restaurant and as we took each other in, I could tell this wasn't exactly a meeting of soul-mates. Picture an edgy, artisty L.A. dude with a ponytail and a satchel over his shoulder meeting a demure navy blue T-shirt dress and strappy sandals woman who looks like somebody's mother. Yeah, not a match. But we still had great conversation and an enjoyable dinner. I met a person and we talked. We never saw each other again and it was OK because it turns out he had three Chihuahuas, which is *so* not my thing.

And that's how these decisions get made. Mismatched clothing styles, three chihuahuas and you're out.

Chances are, the first person you meet isn't going to be "the one" anyway. Another reason to relax. This is your education. If something happens to develop your first time out and you never have to date again, count yourself ridiculously lucky.

What to Talk About

If you've already been texting and talking over the phone to your date, you have a bit of a dialogue going. So with any luck, you can slide into a conversation that follows your last exchange. We bring this up partly because, without some kind of banter having been developed, you'll have to get it going at the date, while you're also dealing with your first impressions, their first impressions, and major nervousness.

I met one guy for a first date who didn't want to talk beforehand, except once to set up the date and chit-chat briefly. He said he didn't believe in having much contact, pre-date. Face-to-face was where it was at, for him. Well, yes, but let's grease the wheels a little.

Anyway, we met, talked coffee small-talk while we ordered, and then sat down. I looked at him. He looked at me. His hands were folded in his lap, and he smiled at me in that way that therapists do, as if to say, "And what brings you here today?" It was completely unnerving and caused me to blurt out some kind of opening question nonsense, to which he gave a very short answer and then smiled that smile again as if waiting for my next offering. I couldn't figure out what his game plan was, but I tried again. It took a lot of effort to get the conversation going, and I soon lost interest. Needless to say, it was a "one and done" first date.

Extroverts may not need any help, but it's a good idea to prep a little about things to ask and bring up on the date. Some conversations lead more naturally to chemistry and connection, while others leave you feeling blah about each other.

- Have some questions ready. Reread their profile or messages to remind you of their interests and anything you'd like to ask about.

- Start light. Ask about their day, chit-chat, but don't be afraid to eventually ask or talk about real-life subjects. Not your deepest, darkest secrets, but, you know, real stuff. What's important to you, what you believe in, challenges you've overcome, family, what your life looks like.

- More than the facts, please. Impersonal conversations about the places you've been and the things you've done aren't the kind that make a warm connection, and they definitely don't lead to chemistry. It's how you *feel* about the people, projects, and challenges in your life that are more likely to create that magic.

- In our experience, questions and discussion about the "exes" will come up during the first date, if they haven't already. Most dating sites say not to talk about exes on the first date, but they're nuts if they believe it won't come up. But keep first-date conversation about exes general; cruise over the highlights (or lowlights) without a blow-by-blow of how and why you broke up. And no spewing of venom. Big hint: It's not really the exes everybody is curious about. What they are really listening for is how you talk about your relationship (avoid judge-y, blame-y, one-sided evaluations), whether you're a bunch of drama, and whether they have to be worried about your ex coming after them.

- Children and grandchildren. This topic will also likely come up on the first date. Resist the temptation to whip out those cute photos of your brood unless you're both really into it, but even then, keep it limited. Those little tykes with missing teeth and fingers up their noses are not as cute to anyone else as they are to you. Especially if your date doesn't have any.

- Red flags. Aside from any other red flags that might pop up, if you find your date is vague or covert about family, their past, their friends, or their job, it may be a sign something is not quite right in Whoville. It might not be anything, but then again, it might. You can choose to keep asking questions, or make a "note to self" to follow up until you're either satisfied or decide to walk away.

- Your attitude is showing. Are all your stories about your successes or how great your life is (egomaniac)? Your failures (low self-esteem)? How much you dislike this or that (judgmental/negative)? Juicy stories about other people (gossip)? A little bit of humility mixed with a little bit of pride mixed with an overall positive attitude and a whole lot of curiosity about the person you're sitting across from goes a long way.

- "What are you looking for?" is a question that frequently comes up during the first date. Yes, some version of it was probably on both your online profiles, but it'll come around again, and is a broad enough topic that there are usually lots of ways to talk about it.

- "Be yourself" sounds like great advice, but you're trying to make a good impression while being relaxed while thinking of what to talk about while also being in the moment, listening attentively and trying to figure out what to order, so yeah. Just do your best.

- Make sure you are communicating *with* a person, not at them or to them. Nobody likes a barrage of questions, even if it does come from your interest in them. It usually ends up sounding like an interview. By the same token, be careful of long monologues about yourself, and notice when their interest wanes on a particular topic. If they nod off, that's a bad sign.

- Some questions are better than others to get conversation going. It's the difference between "Have you ever been to Alaska?" vs. "What kind of travel interests you?" Or "How many children do you have?" vs. "Tell me about your family." "Do you ski?" vs. "How do you like to spend your free time?" Learning how to ask open questions is a skill, and worth the time to develop the ability, especially if having conversations with new people isn't one of your strong points.

First-Date Chemistry

Zap. That spark of electricity; the magical something that happens or doesn't. It's the drumroll in the background of every first date that determines whether there's going to be a second date or it ends up on that growing pile of "nope." Here's the kind of things people say when chemistry happens:

"I felt so comfortable. The conversation flowed."

"I felt like I already knew him/her."

"Neither one of us wanted to end the evening. We closed the restaurant down."

"The goodnight kiss was incredible."

The most common ingredients seem to be ease *(I can be myself)*, familiarity (*We "get" each other*), and a spark *(I'm attracted to him/her)*. Sometimes there's ease and familiarity but no spark, which is one of those mysteries of the universe (or maybe it's that pheromones thing, who knows?).

Whether we're conscious of it or not, as we sit there blabbing about ourselves and taking in our date, we're registering reactions—ours and theirs. We're complicated beings, with histories and hot-buttons and memories and unresolved issues from our screwed-up childhoods (if you didn't have a screwed-up childhood, go in peace; we're happy for you), so every exchange signals us to either peel away another layer of the onion that is us, or keep ourselves protected.

It's scary because it makes us vulnerable, but being willing to let ourselves be seen as less than perfect is more likely to lead to chemistry than those amusing anecdotes about our adventures. Nobody's looking to be rejected after showing who they really are, but if we are willing to reveal a little about our values, personality, and nature, we also increase the chances for a connection to happen.

So about that spark again... Listen up, guys, because this one's for you. There's got to be a little flirtation. Women are conditioned to respond to flirting, but most of us won't initiate it. So say something nice about how she looks, or how she's dressed, how you're enjoying talking with her.

You can also stop the conversation at some point to say something like, "I really like you," "I feel comfortable with you," or whatever. Don't make shit up, though. But if you're appreciating something about the connection, let it out! If she's going to get butterflies, this is when it'll start happening; not when you're telling her that story about your frustrations with your cell phone company or how cold it's been this past winter.

Slightly trickier, but generally safe, is the slightest of physical contact while you're chatting. I said "slightest," guys. A quick touch to her arm to emphasize something you're saying, a brief moment when your knee brushes hers—these are moments when the sparks can start to fly—or not. If she flinches at your touch or moves away, it's not happening, dude.

One guy I was on a first date with did the casual touch thing—while gesturing, he made slight contact with my arm (one of the safest body zones, guys). Each time I felt a zing—yay!—chemistry. He commented on it later, saying something like "…and I realize I've touched your arm several times while we've been talking…," allowing me to flirt back (or not, although I chose to) with, "Yes, I've noticed and I like it." This quickly led to the invitation for a second date.

Which brings up a note for women. Guys are hoping to get some indication of your receptivity and interest in them. Apparently, some of us are cautious to the point of seeming distant; that or we're just hard to read. Eye contact, a smile, anything. Don't keep him guessing. If he brought you flowers, gave you a compliment, or made any other gesture of thoughtfulness, let him know.

Are you having a good time? Is there something you like about him? Tell him. If you don't look interested, it'll probably be a one and done, which is fine if that's what you're after.

Having said all that, you need to figure out how much chemistry you expect and how much time you're willing to give it to develop. Does it have to be fireworks right from the start or it's a no-go?

Debi had a date with a guy who said he knew within the first ten minutes whether he wanted to have a second date with a woman or not (which is a weird thing to say on a first date; we don't recommend it!). Being bold, she asked if the verdict was in on her yet. He said he definitely wanted a second, and even a third date with her and suggested a day for it, to which she agreed. That was the last she ever heard from him. Go figure.

When I was married, I couldn't believe how my single friends, male and female, made snap decisions about a person based on one date. But once you're out there, it makes more sense. However, it's worth considering hanging in there a bit before letting a potentially great partner get away because the first date wasn't exciting enough. Dating services also recommend you go on three dates before deciding whether or not to continue seeing someone.

I decided to try out that theory once with a guy I met online. Our first date was comfortable, easy, fine, but no spark for me. I have no idea if there was for him. He didn't flirt, we didn't kiss. He called me up for a second date, and I said yes. Same thing happened: good conversation, some commonalities and laughing, but flatline as far as the electric grid. He asked me out a third time and I found myself checking my phone and hoping for an emergency so I could leave early. Although I didn't follow up with him, this is one of those connections that can result in a friendship, if both parties are interested.

Basic Dating Etiquette

This stuff is common sense, but if you haven't dated since *The Beatles* were popular, you might need some reminders.

Get there on time. Never a good idea to be late to a date, especially a first one. If you arrive first, scope out a place to sit that's conducive to conversation, if it's a restaurant or café. You know, not right next to the espresso machine.

Ordering. If it's counter service, we recommend that men ask the woman what she'd like and offer to order for her. If a waiter is involved, get that person's attention and order drinks before you start in on conversation.

Short tale of what not to do: I arrived to a first date at a wine bar with counter service. My date was already seated outside with a glass of wine in front of him. Although not the point of this story, the first thing I noticed was how heavyset he was. Quick trip through the mental files reminded me that he'd had no full-body shots online.

We greeted each other, and I sat down. He seemed nervous; I tried to get a conversation going. As he sipped away, oblivious, I dropped a few hints:

"What kind of wine are you drinking?"

"It's the pinot."

A few beats.

"How is it?"

"Pretty good."

I started to wonder which charm school he'd attended. It was now abundantly clear that I was expected to get my own damn wine—or maybe he was just nervous and forgot.

I tried one more time, "I guess I'd better go get myself something to drink," giving him the opportunity to remember his manners.

Crickets.

I went inside to order, fighting the voice inside that said, *Date from hell—escape while you can!* but reined in the impulse and made polite conversation for a torturous half hour or so. As we finished our wine, he asked if I'd like to do this again, but he must've read the "Are you effing kidding me?" look on my face, and quickly added, "Or we can think about it." I'm pretty sure I ran down the stairs. One and done.

Seating. You go in, find a table and sit down, right? Wrong. This is your first real look at each other, your first actual physical nearness. Distance in seating creates emotional safety at the same time it discourages warmth and intimacy. Keeping this in mind, here are some pointers:

Barstools minimize barriers and maximize the possibility of physical contact. Sitting kitty-corner at a table puts you close to each other but with a little furniture between you, while sitting across from each other provides maximum distance but means you have to look directly at each other, which can create uncomfortable staring during the inevitable lulls in conversation.

The absolute worst seating arrangement for intimate conversation is the style with a long booth across the back wall and chairs facing, especially if the tables are close together (like in French restaurants). You're more likely to create a connection with the person next to you instead of your date across the table. Conversations aren't private. Try to avoid this like the plague for first dates.

Sitting outdoors can be a great option. All that fresh air creates a more relaxed atmosphere.

Distractions

- Leave the phone in your pocket or purse. If it's on the table, you're going to look at it. This includes those watches that burp out all your social media messages as they come in, making their wearers look like they have somewhere else to go as they glance down at their latest urgent Facebook update. If you absolutely have to take a call, tell your date why, make it brief, apologize for the interruption—and don't do it twice!

- If the date is not going well or you're losing interest, don't be that guy (or woman, but it's usually the guy), who's got one eye on the game being broadcast on the wall behind her. You might think we can't tell you're watching, but we can.

- Here's the worst one: Debi was on a first date. She excused herself to go to the ladies' room and when she returned, she noticed he had his phone on his lap and was scrolling through profiles on a dating site. Another case of one and done.

Alcohol and Bad Decisions

You know how the more you drink, the funnier everything is? But then the next morning, you're like, *Wait, what did I say/do last night? Oh shit.*

Hopefully by this age, you're aware of your limits and that kind of thing doesn't happen anymore. But it is possible, especially if you're nervous, to swill down a few too many and end up showing a side of yourself that should wait until someone already loves you unconditionally and is willing to gently load you into an *Uber* after an evening of being "overserved."

I've tried to train myself to hear that small voice that says, "You've had two drinks and you're good. More isn't better. Drink water, fool."

It's not only the unfettered self-confessions that tumble out with too much drinking, there's also the loosening of inhibitions that leads too easily to sex on the first date.

So, yeah. Watch out for alcohol.

Who Pays?

Most guys our age(s) say they expect to pay for the first date. These same guys say you'll make points if you at least offer to share the bill or leave the tip. They say they won't accept, but will appreciate it. I'm sure there are others who would be insulted if a woman offered to pay. But it's a good idea to figure out your approach to this before you go on the date, whether you're male or female.

Keeping in mind that many of these first dates are also last dates, after a while the cost really adds up for the men. Some guys have emptied their wallets on first dates ad infinitum, and they might get a little prickly about this.

One guy I dated twice got angry with me when he called for a third date and I declined. The way he figured it, if I knew I wasn't interested after the second date, the polite thing to do would've been to offer to split the bill. I hadn't thought of it until he said that, and I apologized. Live and learn.

I'm a feminist from way back, so I'm slightly uncomfortable making the assumption it's always up to the guy to pay. I usually say "thank you" on the first date and if we keep on seeing each other, a few dates down the road I offer to split or pick up a tab.

Debi, on the other hand, has a more traditional view: a date is when a man takes a woman out. He pays. Period.

One time (after that date where I got chewed out and after I heard from other men that they appreciate a woman at least offering to chip in) I offered to split the bill on a first date. The guy looked mildly disappointed and said, "No, I asked you out, I should pay—unless this is our last date?" Which I didn't mean to imply, but it goes to show that even with the best of intentions, we're all confused and there are no rules you can rely on. Sorry. We know you were hoping for more.

Ending the Date

Glasses are empty, plates have been cleared. You've both made your first impressions and chemistry has either happened or not. Will there be a second date? If you both felt a connection, this part's easy. Yes and yes. If you're both a strong "no," it's also usually simple, except for that awkward last moment of mumbling, "Well, it was nice meeting you," "Uh yeah, bye." But if you're not sure or they're not sure, it can get tricky.

What to Say When It's a "No"?

Here are some polite ways to finish things up and get out of there with a minimum of rejection. You can say something like "I've enjoyed meeting you, but I don't think we're a match," or "I enjoyed meeting you, but I don't think we're looking for the same things." You can also say, "I've enjoyed meeting you," and leave out the rejection message.

The weenie way is to say a bunch of lies like "This was great; let's get together again," "Sure, let's exchange numbers," "I'll text you," when you have no intention of doing so.

Whatever works for you. We support bravery, although we've both been guilty of weenie tactics from time to time. Just be aware that someone may say they're interested or will follow up and then you get the ghosting thing. You thought it was a good connection. When people ghost me, I try to shrug it off. OK, total honesty. Sometimes I lie awake wondering if it was too soon to have told that story about when I took acid in the '70s, or if my hair was sticking out weirdly or oh God, did I forget to thank him for dinner...?

It's not that people are cruel or heartless. Sometimes it's easier and less emotionally painful not to say anything rather than "Hey, you're too boring/arrogant/ditzy/fake/angry for me and I'm not feelin' it, so I won't be going on another date with you. Ciao."

If you can find a neutral way of saying "no," most people will appreciate the honesty. And if someone rejects you, try not to crumple. If it's not a match for them, it's not a match, no matter what you felt. Best not to obsess over it. Move on and start searching again. By the way, remember when we told you it takes time and a thick skin? Yeah, this is what we meant.

Sometimes Debi and I commiserate and help stand each other up again after a date we liked disappears. A friend who understands is a wonderful thing. In fact, we highly recommend finding one who is also dating so you can ask them things like "Am I crazy or was that a dick move?"

If you're finding yourself with lots of first dates but no follow-ups, it may be time to go back to the chapter "Are

You Ready for This?" or some self-reflection about how you might be coming across on the first date.

If you're really, really brave, you might try texting one of the dates and ask them to be brutally honest with you about why there was no second date. Tell them you've accepted it's over, but you're trying to learn from the experience. You might find out something important that you can work on, even if it hurts to hear it. Isn't self-development great?

One More Thing about Ending That First Date...

Saying goodbye. Kiss? Hug? Run as fast as you can in the other direction? How much and whether there is physical contact is a personal choice. But, if they are interested, most guys are trained to go in for some kind of affection-ate gesture as a way of saying goodbye. Others will wait to see how the woman behaves at the goodbye. So be pre-pared for this little moment as you part ways.

Women need to convey what kind of goodbye you're pre-pared for, and men, here's your moment to add up all the signals you gave and got during the date and determine which kind of goodbye to go for.

The quality of the connection should match the type of goodbye. If the date was a dud, it's typically, "Bye, see ya."

Hugs come with a variety of messages—from the tentative, back-pat friendly hug you'd give to your grandma to the full-on body press hug that leaves you both vibrating with sensual pleasure. Kisses, too, convey different signals—from the dry little peck to the ones that scream, "Oh yeah!"

One guy told me he was dating a woman but he wasn't sure where the relationship was going because after three dates, she hadn't shown interest in a kiss. Gotta give signals, people. Words are better. If you like somebody but you aren't ready for kissing, say so. Similarly, to leave open the possibility of a "move," don't jump in your car and drive off.

When I was first starting to date after my divorce, I was clueless about this end-of-date behavior. The date went really well, and when the evening ended, we got to his car first and continued chatting. He offered to drive me to my car but I said, "Oh, that's okay. My car is pretty close." He gently insisted, so I got in. I was going to hop out at the closest intersection in order not to inconvenience him any further, but he asked me to wait while he pulled over to the curb. It wasn't until we parked and he went in for a kiss that I realized he'd been thinking ahead to create the right moment and I was the big Duh.

Staying in Touch

"Do you like me?" "How much do you like me?" These are the questions that linger after a first date with someone you liked.

Now that we're older, we don't have to play that game where you wait three days before contacting each other to prove you're not "needy." The thread of connection is thin and fragile, so send a text, "Really enjoyed our date. Looking forward to seeing you again," or, "Thanks again for a lovely evening," or, "Good morning, thinking of you." People like to know they're on your mind, and sending a message goes a long way toward creating warm fuzzies.

Being busy is not an excuse. Our cell phones are usually planted right next to us, if not velcroed to our foreheads, and a text message takes seconds to write and send. But if you text the person and get no answer, don't keep sending messages. Non-response to a text is generally a sign of ghosting, especially if you haven't agreed to get together again.

"Radio silence" after the first date, even if you already agreed to a second date, can make someone wonder if you're still there and interested. Not only that, but after one date, most people are back online, continuing to search and swipe. If you leave a gap in communication, they may move on.

How often should you text or call after that first date? Everybody has different expectations about what is the "right" amount of communication between dates. What's too much for one person is too little for another. Somebody who is still working may be more pre-occupied and communicate less, whereas for retired people with wide-open days, the desire to reach out may be more frequent.

We'll make a generalization and say women prefer more communication, while men often tend to leave more space between calls and texts. Or as one woman posted online,

> *I'm so over him!*
> *...Hang on, he just texted me back.*
> *Never mind.*
>
> —Author Unknown

As a general rule, don't always be the one to initiate texts or phone calls, and don't overwhelm people with frequency or long, wordy messages.

The Second Date

Second dates are often more nerve-wracking than first dates, at least in our experience. On first dates, you're full of stories and questions. The time fills easily.

Now you need to go a little deeper. It's too early to whip out your skankiest secrets, but be prepared to share a little more and encourage your date to do so as well. Everyone's got their mental scorecard going about whether this connection has relationship potential, so it helps to show a little more of who you are as a way to find out if your values and lifestyles are compatible. The optimism you felt after the first date may not be the same after you venture past the polite behavior of the initial meeting. As one woman wrote online:

> *Me: So I met this guy...*
> *Me: (two days later) Never mind.*

I had a great first date with a guy and was driving to meet him for our second date. An old pro in the dating realm by then, I was surprised to find that the closer I got to my destination, the more nervous I became. There was more riding on this date than the first one, now that we knew we felt something for each other. Would those feelings still be there?

I had way too much time to worry about whether it would be fun, whether he'd still like me, whether I'd still like him, whether I was wearing the right thing, what we'd talk about. (We lived almost two hours apart, so I had a while to torture myself.) I felt the familiar dry mouth and damp armpits setting in. I called Debi for some pre-date intervention. She got right to the point.

"Do you have deodorant with you?"

"No! Why would I drive around with deodorant?"

"Oh my God, girl. You always need to keep deodorant in your car! And get the spray kind."

More stuff nobody ever told me. License, registration, deodorant? With the five minutes or so I had to spare, I begged Google to tell me where the nearest drugstore was, tore ass into a shopping center, ran into the CVS, grabbed gum and deodorant, and dutifully applied emergency personal hygiene in the car before meeting him. I never use spray, though, so I got my usual stick.

The next time Debi was in my car, I proudly showed her

my dating first-aid stash, carefully hidden in the console, but her look told me something was wrong.

"You didn't buy spray. In the summer it's going to melt all over everything." So much to learn, so little time.

The other phenomenon we've experienced on second dates (not that deodorant is a phenomenon of second dates, but you get the drift) is that guys who were previously polite and offered a chaste kiss at the end of the first date, get to the second date and treat it like a hormonal free-for-all.

As guys try to "get some," those old baseball metaphors (first base, second base, etc.) come back to haunt us. What base am I willing to go to and when? Are there rules about this? Why do I feel like I'm fending off my high school boyfriend again?

So be prepared. Second dates—not always what you were expecting.

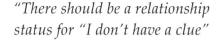

"There should be a relationship status for "I don't have a clue"

The First Relationship Since Your Marriage

Your first relationship after losing a spouse can be a "rebound," especially if you haven't healed from your loss. Rebounds—the way to stuff the hole left by what you lost. Somebody to take care of you while you lick your wounds, or somebody who seems like the complete opposite of your last partner (to help you believe you're not making the same mistake this time).

Emotional caretakers are wonderful when you're hurting. At first these partners distract you from your pain, but once you're emotionally healthier, you want out but now it's more difficult because, well, they took such good care of you when you really needed someone. It's another reason to wait and reflect before jumping into a new relationship.

This is also a warning to those who get involved with someone who is fresh out of a relationship. They may treat you like the answer to their prayers, until suddenly one day you're not.

Dating More Than One Person at a Time

This is where online dating gets a little crazy. You may have more than one date lined up in a week. It's dizzying and exciting to be going on multiple dates in a short period of time, but it's also confusing. Who did you tell what to? Whose stories are whose? There's likely going to be a lot of "Did I already tell you this?"

Likewise, I find myself re-asking questions like "So how many kids do you have?" and then realize he's the guy who doesn't have any kids.

One guy with whom I'd had a pretty good first date was putting my information in his phone to get in touch later and he said, "It's Linda, right?" And of course my name's not Linda, but we had a good laugh over it.

At times, Debi has had her dates lined up like a conveyer belt. Not because she wanted to date the multitudes, but because she'd been hurt too many times by becoming exclusive too quickly, only to find that the relationship didn't last.

You have a choice. You can stop responding to anyone else once you've had a date with one person and intend on seeing them again. It's a more sane approach, but less efficient.

Most of us are looking for that one-on-one relationship that works for the long haul and takes us off the online dating sites forever. There are many ways to get there, so do whatever floats your boat.

Beware the Impossible Composite Person

No, there's not some lumbering "Composite Person" ready to jump out of the bushes at you. This one is in your head. Remember the Chinese menu? I'll have one from Column A, one from Column B, and one from Column C.

Once you've met and dated several people, you get clearer about what you're looking for, but you liked this one's sense of humor, you preferred that one's sharp mind/ affectionate style/personality/body/pick your favorite combo and pretty soon you're waiting for perfection.

I used to work in real estate, and buyers did this all the time with houses. "I really love the kitchen from that last house, but I want the yard from the other one, and I really love the architecture of this house and could I have it all for the price of that fixer-upper we saw last week?" Dream on. Or actually, get real.

It's human nature to make comparisons, but once a relationship is over, it's better to concentrate on the person you're currently with. You're not likely to find Mr. or Ms. Perfect, but if you're lucky, you'll find someone you love and who loves you (and you can both handle the weight of the other's baggage).

And Now, a Word about Players

Guys are welcome to correct us if we're wrong here, but we are going to assume for the moment that when we refer to "players," we mean men. Players have always been with us in the dating world, but Internet dating has provided a bonanza for these guys, who can now select from the human buffet on a daily basis.

It would be great if we knew which ones they were, but they lie. They say they are looking for a serious relationship. They say they are tired of "dating." They are usually very good at sweeping you off your feet ("I've never met anyone like you"; "This is so different/special/amazing"). They can flirt like nobody's business. They can convince you this is the "it" you've been looking for, only to pull the ol' ghost trick after a few dates, or after they've gotten you into bed, whichever comes first.

If red flags don't warn you, the only way to really know if you have a player is to give it time and not get too excited by that first or second date. Players desire you but they don't love you, although it might feel the same at first.

My Aching Back

Ah, aging. It gives us so many romantic things to deal with. But seriously, at some point near the beginning of dating, people should tell one another about any health issues they have. Those battle scars from life, major and minor. You've got your allergies (cat, perfume, particular foods), your arthritis, Crohn's disease, bad back, bum knee, chronic pain, and bouts with cancer, to name a few.

> *Forget the cute smile or the toned body. Show me a picture of your medicine cabinet, so I know what I'm really getting into.*
>
> — Author Unknown

We're going to get a little serious here for a moment. One of the toughest issues in starting an intimate relationship at this age is imagining the caretaker role for one or the other of you, which could happen at any moment, no matter how healthy you both are right now. It's a sobering thought.

It's one thing to be with a partner for years, decades; to have a bond that's developed over time, to have had your experience running carefree through that meadow holding hands, and then to face the health issues associated with aging. It's quite another to take on that responsibility with someone you've just met. We don't have a solution for this, except to hope you have years before any serious health issues occur. If they or you have a serious health issue right off the bat, it can easily affect the decision about whether move forward with the relationship.

Retired or Not Retired

People retire at all ages, and some people work until the day they die. If you've lived with someone for years and one of you retires, it can be challenging, but you already have a relationship established. Availability for dating isn't an issue.

But it's really hard to develop a new relationship when one person works and the other one doesn't. First of all, the person with the job isn't around for all that fun daytime stuff and might be tired when they're off work. Depending on the type of employment, they usually can't get away for spontaneous road trips or other kinds of travel. Your energies and lifestyle are very different.

For many retirees, it's a deal-breaker if a potential date has a full-time job. But if you're that retiree, make sure you're not excluding someone who may have a very flexible job or one where they can set their terms or hours.

Widows/widowers vs. Divorced People

If we were going to make a generalization about the main difference between divorced people and widows/widowers, it would be this: divorced people aren't carrying around a whole bunch of sentimental feelings about their ex; widows/widowers often are.

There are plenty of exceptions, but it's good to know how the two are likely to be different. Divorced people, as a whole, don't bring up their exes that much, unless they've become friends or have children together and still interact with each other. But they've moved on emotionally (or they should have), and the relationship they once had is clearly in the past.

The exception to this are divorced people who are still pissed at their ex and take every opportunity to rant about them. These people are not quite ready to start a new relationship and should sit quietly and contemplate life for a bit longer. I was probably guilty of that when I first started dating, and I scared one guy away when I told the story (which I thought was hilarious) about how I threw my wedding album out with the trash. We'd been having a great conversation but with that story, this look came over his face and I never heard from him again.

Widows and widowers have gone through a very different kind of pain and loss than divorced people. Those of us who've divorced lived through phases of estrangement, arguing, and deterioration in our previous marriages or partnerships—not to mention the divorce process, which has a knack for turning your ex into the pig beast from hell.

Widows/widowers have lost someone they were in love with, or at least still wanted to be with. Their grief is deeper, often paralyzing, and their desire to "get over it" is not the same as it is for most divorced people.

Debi and other widow/widowers we've talked to recognize they needed more help moving on and opening their hearts to love again. She was very young when her second husband and father of her youngest child died. It was six weeks from his diagnosis to his death, leaving her alone with their five-year-old and two children in their teens. She went to support groups and leaned on friends, but with children to raise, she felt forced to put her head down and push forward.

After a while, she tried dating but found herself struggling to relinquish control. She felt if she relied completely on herself and held the reigns tight enough, she could move through her days, raise her family, and survive. She soon realized she wasn't ready to let anyone in and had to take a step back and work on herself. It was a four-year journey that eventually included PTSD treatment to deal with her emotional paralysis. Then she was finally able to date again and find her next partner.

Another widower said he had to learn that it wasn't about letting go of his loved one, which he wasn't prepared to do, but learning to open himself to love again.

And yet another said his dying wife had already picked out his next wife for him. Whatever their deal was, he started dating three months after her death and felt ready.

So if you're dating a widow/widower, be prepared that the person may lovingly bring up their late spouse in conversation, and they will always hold a special place in their heart for that person. It doesn't matter if it was two years ago or twenty, the late spouse will always be there in some form or other, so if you're going to get involved with a widow or widower, you'll need to accept this.

A word to the widows and widowers: while you are holding that special place, you won't find love again unless you actually make room in your life and open your heart to new possibilities. You need to go through a different kind of grieving process. No one will ever take your late spouse's place, but a heart is a wonderful thing—it's got lots of room for more love, if you let it.

The Third Date and Beyond

So let's say you had about six dates with different people that went nowhere, then you met this seventh person and without warning, your body perked up, sparks zapped in your veins, and emotions flew off the charts. You go on several dates in quick succession because it feels so good, and then time does a warp thing and you're like, "*Wow, I feel like I've known you forever,*" when actually it's only been about five minutes.

After a stream of previous dates that ended in "No, nope, maybe sorta but then, no," and "I felt something but I never heard from them again," you can become over-stimulated by one that makes you feel like you've hit the jackpot.

You're so comfortable together, you're certain this person is the one. "*Surely, this is it. I haven't felt like this in a really long time, we're perfect for each other,*" etc. Sorry to be cynical if you're feeling love, but we've both fallen into this particular rabbit hole more than once over the course of dating and all we have to say is watch out for that other shoe. It *will* drop, eventually. Not that you shouldn't enjoy those lovely tingly feelings—just be careful of thinking you have the whole picture just because it's so good at the beginning.

Hard as it might be to believe when you're in the middle of being swept up, as time goes on, new issues, red flags, and baggage will show up, both yours and theirs. You may become closer or you may become ambivalent, but there absolutely will be more parts to the picture than appeared at first.

Three dates into it is a good time for a first evaluation. Have a check-in with your gut, heart, and head. If you're a romantic, your heart will be jumping up and down screaming, "Yes, yes, yes!" so put it over in the corner for a time-out while you have a little chat with the other systems.

Any cause for concern? All systems go? Maybe one or two niggly little things but hey, nothing's perfect? How's the baggage situation? Are you starting to think of this as a relationship? Are you exclusive? Have you been physically intimate yet? Sometimes emotions cool way down after the first sexual encounter because of the tension that built up to the "event." Other times, it propels you forward.

Oh and a note to guys—listen up, this one's important: When you have sex with her for the first time, *text or call her* ASAP after you go home and say something sweet. Don't ask why, just do it.

Are We in a Relationship Now?

> *"I'm at the age where dating is like:*
> *'Are we doing this or not?'*
> *Because otherwise, I've got lots of other*
> *shit I need to be doing."*
>
> —Author Unknown

Visiting Each Other's Homes

AT SOME POINT, you will visit each other's homes. (If they never bring you to where they live, be on the lookout—red flags flying overhead.)

First the safety issues, primarily for women—unless men

tell us there really are *Fatal Attraction* bunny-boiling women out there.

If you're going to a guy's house, at least give a friend his address and full name, and when you're going. Text your friend when you're home safely (or if you decide to stay over!).

My daughter once called me while I was on my way to visit a man at his house for the first time. It was our third date and I was confident he wasn't an axe murderer, although he lived in a rather remote area. When she heard where I was going, she went all parental on me:

"Mom, you should always drop a pin!" she said. Feeling like the irresponsible kid (which happens often since I've become single), I reassured her I was OK and told her the guy's address. By the way, if you want to annoy the younger generation, try giving them information verbally instead of electronically. "I don't have a pen, Mom. Text it to me." Her voice told me she was shaking her head at my stone-age approach to information exchange.

If you've never heard of this pin-dropping thing, it has something to do with online maps and phone apps and identifying where you are and then somehow conveying all this to someone else. Sounds like too many steps to me.

Our home reflects our personality and lifestyle, and

anyone who is considering a long-term relationship is asking themselves, "Could I live here?" or "Could I live like this?" When a date comes to your house to visit you, they're viewing you in your natural habitat for the first time, and let's admit it, most of us go a little feral when we live alone.

This is the first date for your home, so a little sprucing up is in order. Are there fresh towels and did you make sure there aren't any stray hairs in the sink of any bathroom they might use? And how about that plate in the living room with the half-eaten toast?

Also, you are the host and they are your guest. Since I don't cook much for myself, my freezer typically contains a Trader Joe's pizza and a bottle of vodka, with vitamins, withered limes, and a nearly empty jar of salsa in the fridge section. Consider a trip to the store for a few guest-worthy snacks and adult beverages.

Doing the Long-Distance Dance

We warned you, right? But you went and did it anyway. Maybe at first, dating someone who lives an hour away doesn't seem like a big deal. But then it is. Whether it's a one-hour drive or a four-hour plane flight, they both set you up for long-distance issues.

Personally, I wouldn't go for really long-distance; it's way too expensive and hard to maintain. The longest long-distance I ever did was with my ex-husband, who lived eight hours away by car when we first met online, and ended up with more than his share of speeding tickets until he moved to my town. But we felt enough of a connection through our very frequent emails and infrequent phone calls (remember, at the dawn of time, there was no texting and long-distance calling costs were significant) that we made it happen, and it's what will determine if your long-distance relationship has any chance at success. The strength of the connection, that is. And an intention for one of you to move, if it works out.

- **Where do you meet?**

   One of you comes to the other? Meet halfway? The driving, no matter who does it, gets old really fast. And because of all the driving, the dates tend to be longer than local dates. After all, you've traveled and you have nowhere else to go, nothing else to do but be with each other.

   My first long-distance date lasted six hours (we had agreed to meet in a town halfway between us and go for a walk, which went well, so we decided to go have a drink, which went well, so we decided to have dinner together).

   Our second date lasted twelve hours—same reason. We spent the day together, had dinner, and then went to listen to a band at a local club. Luckily, "halfway" was a town where each of us had family, so we weren't forced to pay for hotels. After several dates of meeting in the middle, we started visiting each other's homes.

- **Nix the spontaneity**

  It's tough with long distance to say, "Hey, why don't you come over for dinner tonight?" or "Let's go for a walk." You're giving that up, although you can both drive halfway if you don't live too far away from each other.

- **If one or both of you are working**

  This can put a real crimp in a long-distance relationship, because the working person can't get away as easily. So unless you're both retired or one has a very flexible schedule, long-distance dating may not be for you. Debi, who is still in her earning years, has tried several long-distance relationships, with the same result. Not enough time/availability to make it happen. Being retired, I've had more luck with this kind of relationship.

- **Visiting vs. dating**

  Here's what a typical date looks like: somebody picks somebody up, or you meet somewhere, you do something together, and then you go home. Two to four hours, max. Here's what a long-distance date looks like: somebody comes to your town or you go to theirs. You have some kind of plans. You go do them. It takes about two to four hours. Then what? The visitor is still there.

Once the two of you have been to every tourist attraction in your town, then what? And maybe after eight hours together, you're ready for a little break. How do you do that? Is it OK to take a nap when your online date is in town?

- **Sleeping arrangements**

   The elephant in the room. Whether you've met in neutral territory, or one person is visiting the other, what happens at the end of the evening? Get a hotel? Is there a guest room? Or what about that other option? Have you talked about this before visiting? Have you talked about sex yet? Or are you going to avoid the whole topic until you're both exhausted and have copious amounts of wine coursing through your system? Guess what happens then?

   Case in point: I was having a third date with a man who lived about two hours away. We both declared, before my arrival, that there would be no sex. I'd stay in his guest room and we'd spend the time getting to know each other better.

   Upon arrival, I put my suitcase in the guest room. We went out and enjoyed the day, followed by a lovely dinner. There was wine. When we returned to his house, he suggested we watch something on Netflix. The TV was in his bedroom. No biggie. We could handle this. Upshot? I never saw the inside of the guest room again. The relationship was short-lived and I regretted the too-soon intimacy.

I realize this doesn't make my point at all. We had a plan. We just didn't stick to it. I blame the wine. And Netflix. Netflix in the bedroom, especially. Terrible combination.

- **Pacing**

    A long-distance relationship can create intensity very quickly or it can feel glacially slow, depending on how often you're in contact with each other and how often you get together. Relationships need contact in order to develop, and a long-distance one needs special attention to make that happen. If you can't get together frequently, phone calls and texting can go a long way to keep the connection. Face-time calls are better, although it's less than satisfying to hug your phone goodnight. Nothing works as well as actual bodies in the same room at the same time.

    If you visit frequently and/or for long periods, the pace quickens, with intensity and familiarity right on its heels. "Hosting" and "entertaining" can slide too easily into something like "faux living together" as you get comfortable in each other's homes and become more a part of each other's daily life.

If you get along well in the "faux" situation, it can launch you more quickly to a "next steps" conversation. On the flipside, if you don't like it, the whole extended visiting thing can launch you more quickly to realizing this isn't the relationship for you. And we're into saving time here, right?

- **Where do I live again?**

  Another factor in long distance is that, after visiting for a while, you lose your center of gravity. Visiting someone in another town is like being on vacation, which is great except for those pangs of guilt about how you're ignoring your real life.

  Returning home finds you standing in the middle of your living room scratching your head about what exactly you were doing before you left and wondering how to pick up the pieces and find your groove again. And how much groove should you bother getting into, if you're going to take off again? So maybe you pay some bills, check in with friends you've abandoned, put some food in the refrigerator (but not too much, because, you know, you're leaving again soon).

After not very long, this all becomes very disorienting, which is why long-distance relationships are such a bitch.

- **The Endgame**

  From the moment you start a long-distance relationship, the question in the background is, What will we do if things work out? Who's moving where? Your town? Their town? Somewhere new together? What about existing work, family, and social connections? But when do you bring it up?

  Ideally, the conversation should happen early on, before strong feelings develop because what if there's no viable plan to be together and you have to break up and then we're right back at grieving a loss? On the other hand, if you start talking too soon about moving in together you tend to freak people out.

  There are always those super-subtle questions like "How do you like my awesomely cute town?" or "How much fun are you having living out of a suitcase?" Or you could be straightforward and ask, "So have you thought about what to do if this works out?" Not on the first date, though.

Nakedness and the Aging Body

Oh my God, you mean I have to take my clothes off? We may have gotten comfortable with our aging bodies in our old relationship, but to imagine it with someone new is a whole different kind of exposure. Sagging this and crepey that, wrinkles and creases and skin tags, oh my!

We're going to guess women are more self-conscious about this old-body-nakedness thing than men. Most guys seem to have no problem waltzing around the house stark naked in broad daylight, no matter what they look like, and we are in awe of such lack of self-consciousness.

And though we women are finally getting to an age where we care much less than we used to about what other people think of us, we've been conditioned to feel judged on the basis of our looks since we could speak. Now that we've aged, gravity has had its way with us, plus our mid-sections typically bear the ravages of pregnancy and childbirth and our hormones deserted us back at menopause, so this is a sensitive frontier.

For most of our lives, women have spent small fortunes on make-up, moisturizers, facials, hair styling, perms, highlighting, brow waxing, lip waxing, eyelash enhancement—the list is endless. And as we've aged, some have gone the route of cosmetic procedures and enhancements—boob jobs, lipo, filler, Botox, facelifts, hair extensions, brow lifts, laser peels, eyelid lift, lip plumping, tummy tucks, body sculpting, vaginal rejuvenation—all in the name of staving off aging and remaining appealing in our youth-obsessed culture.

Many of us, however, have not done any of these things, preferring to fly our gray hair and sagging-body flag proudly. And what we get for this is guys saying, "Wow, Jane Fonda looks amazing and she's eighty." As if she got there naturally, and now that's the new measuring stick for the rest of us. So guys, try not to add pressure with all those statements about wanting us to be "sexy" at this age; we already try way harder than you do.

Whether male or female, it's up to you, your wallet, and your sensibilities if you choose to get any of these age-deniers, but as Debi says, "Do guys have any idea what it takes to keep this shit afloat?"

If you decide to go with your natural self, we still suggest that you (both genders) get in shape, eat healthy, stay active, and maybe ease into the nakedness thing with some romantic low lighting.

But we're not done. There's the whole landscaping/manscaping issue. Personally, I'm glad my generation got a free pass on this "mow all the hair off yourself" phenomenon, but some younger and big-city folks subscribe to it in one version or another. Chest hair, back hair, bush hair (and ass hair, which I don't even like to think about) is apparently an affront to some people these days. (Excuse us if you're from a place where this isn't a thought. Feel free to skip over this section, in fact).

Debi was talking on the phone once with a man she was considering meeting for a date. At one point, he asked her what her manicure practices were, which struck her as odd. But she started telling him about her favorite nail salon only to realize that he was referring to a different region of her body. So *that* date didn't happen.

But at least be prepared that you might see something you didn't expect, or not see something you *did* expect when the clothes come off.

And if you're a woman wondering whether you should do anything down there, men we asked said they either don't care at all, they prefer it natural, or "Go ahead and do it if you want, but don't give me stubble." Ew.

All we're really saying here is getting naked with a new person and aging bodies might feel weird at first, but it gives us a new way to practice self-acceptance. And if you're not there yet, there's always the low lighting thing.

Sex

Such a small word for such a big deal.

If you've come out of a long marriage, chances are the sex had dwindled, become habitual and less passionate, or dried up altogether. (If not, lucky you!) If so, you may be surprised to find that, once you become single again, those urges come flooding back with a vengeance. It makes you feel more alive, more vital, but it does present a few, uh, problems you might need to address.

OK, so let's get to it. So much to say here. There's the physical side of sex—the workings, shall we say, and then there's the emotional side, the intimacy, the deeper meaning. And the all-important question of when to "do it."

We already mentioned STDs, so if you haven't had that conversation yet, you better take care of it before sex actually happens. And like, not *right* when it's happening. An STD talk while you've got your hands all over each other and clothes are coming off is, let's just say, bad timing.

As far as "how to," you can come right out and say something like, "Before we become intimate (or have sex) I need to know if you've been tested."

Make sure you have a condom, if you're going to use one. And guys, if you haven't used one in thirty years, get some practice before the moment arrives. Picture the awkwardness, otherwise.

We all need to tell each other what we like and how we like it. You've had years of practice with your ex; now you're starting all over. But find the right time and place.

Nothing says buzzkill like yelling, "A little to the left!" while you're thrashing under the sheets.

We're going to be quite blunt in this next statement, so make sure the kids are out of the room—grown-up ones included. My adult daughter recoils at the idea that her aging mother might be having sex at all, and I'm sure she's not interested in the delicate issues involved in it. If you're younger than fifty and reading this, you too may have fewer nightmares if you skip this section. Plenty of time to find out about this stuff later.

So let's just say it: she's dry and his dick doesn't work like it used to. The good news is there are many ways around this, and many options for overcoming most malfunctions. Vitamin supplements, devices, prescriptions, and over-the-counter products. Seek them out. Not to sound like a TV commercial, but talk to your doctor. Hopefully, you and your significant other can figure out a way to talk about whatever issue you're facing and resolve it so you can have intimacy that's mutually satisfying.

Oh and speaking of this, you might find orgasms are more elusive than they once were, and certain positions are no longer achievable or comfortable. So if the man is having trouble getting it up, and/or the woman can't get to orgasm, relax and let each other off the hook. Cuddle for a while. Sexual intimacy at this age—well, it ain't what it used to be.

Now, having gotten that out of the way, let's talk about the implications of when to add sex to your burgeoning romance. When is the right time to do it?

It seems that even at this age, guys are interested in sex anytime, the same as it was when we were all younger. The whole concept that men are led around by their dicks even has a name. After orgasm, a man supposedly has a few minutes of clarity in which he is free of sexual desire and can think with his head. After that, the dick takes over again. If you don't believe us, Google "kenjataimu" (the Japanese word for this phenomenon).

Many women are also experiencing a resurgence of sexual interest, but we feel like we're supposed to be the guardians of the gate, so to speak. But wait, *are* we in high school? What are the rules, now that we're older, supposedly wiser, and no longer have a curfew?

Chemistry propels us forward with great speed toward sex. Not to mention that inner teenager who's taken over your mind and body (*Why wait? You know you want to*, it says). As women, we get more out of sex when there's an emotional connection. Guys, well, *kenjataimu*. As a general rule, we think it's better to wait before jumping into bed. But, "Wait until when?" is the question of the day. Your call.

Debi has a work associate in his sixties who knew we were writing this book. He was out on a first date and called her at 10:00 one night, frantic. She thought it was a work emergency, but instead he said, "What should I do? I'm with a woman who says she doesn't want to have sex right away but we can't keep our hands off each other." Like Debi was now the 24/7 dating hotline for confused seniors. But it makes the point that none of us are sure what to do or when to do it.

And by the way, having sex doesn't necessarily mean you've taken your relationship to the "next level," although it might. But don't start planning any weddings. There are enough situations where sex happened and then the relationship was over. And not because the sex was bad. The sex happened because there was all this chemistry, but not much else.

We probably don't need to say anything about the kind of sex that involves soulful love and a deep connection, the yummy kind that engages you mentally, physically, spiritually and emotionally. We just wanted to warn you that the question of sex may come up (oh, let's cut to the chase, sex *will* come up) before there's love and you have to figure out when you're ready and sort through all the feelings you have about what "ready" means to you. Another good area for an intimate talk.

Becoming Exclusive and Taking Down Your Profiles

Some people call it "having the conversation." When do you decide you're going to be exclusive? Do you wait until you're ready to make a commitment? Or when you decide to focus on this one relationship to see where it goes? Did you have "the conversation" or are you assuming exclusivity?

There's nothing worse than checking in on the website to find your paramour out there on the daily matches when you thought you were both finished shopping (although the question arises, "What were *you* doing back on the website in the first place?")

I've been involved in two rather unpleasant discussions with two separate men as a result of this; one where he swore he'd taken down his profile, yet there it was, and one where I thought I'd taken mine down but had only canceled my membership renewal contract. And Debi, too, thought she'd taken her profile down and her guy accused her of being online. So it's an issue, people.

We need to say here that most of the dating sites make it difficult to hide or take your profile down and/or to cancel your membership. Not to be unkind to the dating sites, but it's to their benefit to have as many profiles up there for prospective clients as possible, to make it look like there are lots of choices.

So you have to figure out where, amidst the drop-downs, the many buttons and various menus, that your options to cancel are buried, and canceling your membership in most cases does *not* hide your profile—it only means they won't automatically renew your contract. Even once your contract is up and you stop paying, your profile will be visible unless you specifically take it down.

After several attempts, plus help from a friend to erase me from *Match.com*, I was told my photo was still up. I wrote the company an email to find out why, and discovered there's not one, not two, but *three* completely separate steps for getting unglued from the site: hide your profile, stop emails, and cancel your subscription.

Some websites will let you hide your profile, but the minute you go back on the site again for any reason, they automatically post your profile again. Word to the wise.

Introducing Your New Relationship to Your Friends and Family

Even before you introduce your new person to your world, you're going to get the questions. "Are you meeting anyone?" "How's it going?" Everyone, it seems, is fascinated by the phenomenon of online dating.

Be prepared that married people will try to live vicariously through you and your dates (while secretly being relieved that they're not having to date at this age), and friends will expect progress reports on the latest online interactions. "Are you still seeing so-and-so?" "When are we going to meet him/her?" The pressure is pretty much exactly like the grilling your parents used to give you as you headed out the door on Friday night.

You can always try to avoid telling anyone you're dating at all, but then it's hard to answer the "What've you been up to?" questions without walking a huge circle around this activity that is taking up a bunch of your waking hours.

It's not fun showing up alone all the time to events, but once you make that introduction, get ready; your relationship will be fair game for more ongoing, prying questions. "Is it getting serious?" "Are you talking about the future?" And the ever-present "Where's so-and-so?" when you show up without them. Friends and family mean well, but what's the deal here? I mean, I don't ask them on a regular basis how their marriage is doing.

I once had a conversation with a casual friend (who's been married for eons and trust me, married people at our age don't get the dating world *at all*) who'd met my current flame at a social function. Next time I saw the friend, I was alone. He asked, "Where's so-and-so?" and I had to say, "We're not seeing each other anymore." He looked confused. "But I saw you together last week." Yup, you did. And now it's over. Can we talk about something else now, please?

Friends and family get attached, have opinions, and try to give you advice. "I don't think he's right for you," or "We really liked her. Why did you break up?" Or, "Why don't you give him/her another chance?" Your private life can become uncomfortably public.

Not only that, if you end up introducing multiple prospective partners to your friends and family, your people may start to keep their distance emotionally from your dates, so it's a good idea to set some boundaries with regard to how and when you introduce someone to your world.

Kids

Kids, the most darling type of baggage we have, but baggage nonetheless. They come with you, whether they live with you or not. Your relationship with them is part of the package that is you.

People who don't have kids have the baggage of not understanding what it's like to have kids. There are many people in online dating land who won't consider someone who has never had kids, believing that a childless person is missing a crucial nurturing gene or something. Frankly, we don't subscribe to that; we've met plenty of people who are childless and extremely warm and loving. But fair or not, if you've never had kids, you might be overlooked by parental types.

A suggestion: if you've never had kids but don't want to be blacklisted because you actually love kids and have some close family relationships with kids, maybe mention in your profile something about all those great nieces and nephews whom you adore. It could make someone reconsider.

For those of us with kids, no matter what age, expect them to have separate and distinct reactions to this phenomenon of their parent dating again. Your kids may have loyalties to their other parent, be protective of your getting hurt, and/or be jealous of some stranger taking away your attention.

Expect everything from the twelve-year-old who eyes you suspiciously with, "Who is this *friend* of yours and why are they in my house?" to your twenty-six-year-old son who keeps his earbuds in so he doesn't hear anything, to your thirty-something daughter who wrote your profile and is desperate to marry you off.

It's obviously more of a big deal to bring someone home when you're raising children. I briefly dated one widower who brought me home on the third date to have dinner. I assumed he would have made arrangements for his thirteen-year-old son to be somewhere else, but nope, my date and I made dinner together while his kid did his homework on the nearby computer, then we all sat down together to eat. I was totally uncomfortable, and couldn't imagine the child felt any better about it.

As for adult children, some are very curious about what you're up to; others don't want to hear about it or be introduced unless it becomes an important relationship. And then there are the ones who act like your strict parents, demanding to know where you're going, with whom, and when you'll be home.

My daughter expects full names and addresses whenever I'm going to a man's house, along with frequent updates on who I'm dating and how it's going. If she lived with me, I'm sure I'd have a curfew.

Money, Again

OK, so now we're down the road and the date has blossomed into a relationship. You may or may not have already sorted out who pays for what, but if you haven't, this is a good time to have that discussion.

There are two camps: those who assume men pay for dates, and those who expect expenses to be shared—in some way, to some extent. Tons of gray area. If you've managed to get on the same page about money intuitively or with minimal discussion, great. But if you aren't sure, you may find the man paying the bills but resenting it or worse yet, having to make a total mood-killing comment like "Hey, you wanna pick up the tab this time?"

And then there's the issue of not knowing how much either of you can afford, or how you like to spend your money, splurging, all that stuff. Money, our values about it, how much we have, how we spend it or don't—is always near the top of the list for problems in couple relationships. The chat you have at this point is practice for if and when the relationship goes the distance.

Uh, oh. Something's Not Right

> *"Dating is just hanging out with someone until you figure out you don't actually like them."*
>
> —Author Unknown

Head, Heart, Gut: Those Talking Body Parts

SOMETIMES WE DEVELOP a connection with someone, and we've moved from dating to having a relationship, but things aren't quite lining up. There are so many reasons for this: Are we looking for perfection? Is our head saying, "No," but our heart is afraid to let go of the relationship? Our gut's going, "This doesn't feel right" but our head's saying, "Don't be so fussy!" The body parts start arguing with each other. It's a jungle in there.

You're ambivalent.

Should I keep going with this?

Does the good outweigh the bad?

Can we both make adjustments?

Am I giving up too much of who I am or am I being too set in my ways?

Is a break-up inevitable and I should leave now before I get another minute older?

It can be difficult to mention these feelings, but if you're unsure, chances are the other person is too. The three-part harmony of head, heart, and gut in agreement indicate you're on the right track. Other than that, we recommend bringing up whatever doesn't feel right.

The Glitch

At first, it's all lovely—the wine flows and there's endless laughing, sunsets, romance, candlelight, the infamous cuddling with Netflix—everything everybody ever said they were dreaming about, you two have together. You can talk about anything, you've been to each other's houses, the sex is great, what could go wrong?

Then something happens. A small something that you ignored at first starts bugging you more. Or they drop some new information on you, like a health problem or the fact that they're not quite totally fully divorced yet. Or one of you starts to withdraw, just the tiniest bit. It may be after a month, it may be more or less, but this is often when The Glitch happens, and you both find out there's more behind the curtain.

Under stress, we deteriorate to a more primitive version of ourselves, the "fight or flight" response. Another side of our personality comes out and before you know it, you're sulking with your arms crossed or they let loose with a nasty comment.

Learning to communicate like a grown-up while pissed off is one of those life skills we can always get better at, and this is a reminder that you or your prospective, formerly perfect-until-this-moment new partner may have a stressful moment that threatens your budding relationship, but it's also a moment to start learning how to fix things between you.

The Adult Conversation

"Yes, well thank you for saying that. I realize now that I wasn't taking your feelings into consideration."

"Thank you. I feel much better since we've cleared the air. And I'll work on bringing things up when they're bothering me instead of bottling it up."

—Kiss, kiss, hug. All better.

The *Actual* Conversation

"You're not the boss of me/don't be so thin-skinned/why do you have to be so negative all the time?/are you ever happy?/picky, picky picky!"

"You big meanie/don't you think of anybody besides yourself?/You're such a narcissist!/I'm going home."

—Slam.

Relationships can succeed or fail based on how you handle differences. If you want to improve your personal conflict style, you can learn these skills. Books, therapy, classes—anything! Your relationship depends on it.

ADD and FOMO

Let's say you've been dating one person and it's going great. But every morning you get these zings and pings and emails declaring that you have twenty-four new matches, BOJO would love to meet you, WHATAGAL likes you, or "HotRudy" in Redondo Beach is into you. Their photos are right there, smiling at you. Some of them are attractive. But you're happy. You don't answer. Are you tempted? Do you have one eye on those new online faces?

If you meet someone you like, but you're curious about who might pop up tomorrow, you could be afflicted with Dating ADD. We're sort of kidding here, but we're sort of not.

Online dating can create a tendency to search without ever landing. Dating sites are designed to be addicting, not to actually help you find someone and get out of there. Where's the money in that?

You've got to realize when what you are looking for is standing right in front of you. Do you know when you're happy, when you've found someone special? How happy do you have to be to stop looking online for someone new? FOMO, anyone? (*Fear Of Missing Out*, in case you don't have anyone around under fifty to explain it to you.)

Or let's say you take your profile down. The dating sites aren't happy about this. They start sending you emails, telling you there are now thirty-seven people waiting to meet you, if you will come back.

Your new relationship hits a bump in the road, and you're upset. You get another email, telling you "waiting4luv" is dying to meet you. Maybe "waiting4luv" is the one. Maybe "waiting4luv" won't upset you like the person you're with now. Maybe they will be more perfect for you. It can become very compelling to get back on. You know, just to look.

Resist the machine! It would love to suck you back in to fantasyland, where photos and profiles promise an ever-more perfect match for you.

Timeline Theories

We have some theories about how relationships change over time, from experiences we and others have had. We offer them for your consideration because we've noticed a pattern.

The first is the "one-month" theory; that perfect phase we talked about earlier, before any glitches show up. You close down your online profiles and start seeing each other exclusively. You see more of each other, you reveal more about yourself, you think of yourselves as "in a relationship." And then the glitch happens, around the one-month mark, and the relationship moves from being perfect to having to deal with each other's actual selves—you know, life complete with baggage.

How you come through the first and subsequent glitches can result in you both becoming closer or starting to question the relationship. You thought you were in love, but suddenly crazy stuff starts banging around in your head.

"Cold feet" happens at all ages, but later in life there is so much more to consider and besides, we don't need each other the way we did when it was time to make babies and start careers. Some thoughts that signal you've stumbled into the land of cold feet:

Maybe I would rather live by myself.

I've already been divorced. I'm afraid to fail again.

Do I really want to take on their baggage? I have enough of my own.

Should I make a commitment if I'm ambivalent?

Let's give ourselves some credit. We've been through a lot by this age; many of us are looking for simplicity, and there's nothing simple about an intimate relationship. But then there's that love and companionship thing. Hmmm.

If you're unsure, you can try taking a break to let a little dust settle. And if you take a break, don't forget to have a talk about whether you're going back online or not.

Massive misunderstandings can occur when one person believes, "We're separated, I can do whatever I want," while the other is thinking, "We're taking a moment, but we're still together."

Then there's the six-month theory. It's really simple: Don't make any big life decisions until six months. No moving in, no engagements. You may be tempted; time is ticking, you're older and wiser now, you shouldn't have to wait if the relationship feels right. And you don't—we've already established that you're a grown-up and you make your own rules.

Not to imply six months necessarily gets you to a decision point; we're just saying it's a nice minimum and a useful landmark to assess your relationship and decide whether to continue to a commitment.

We've met enough daters to hear plenty of stories of how they dated someone for a year, sometimes a couple of years before deciding it wasn't what they wanted. The relationship became comfortable and familiar and the thought of moving on meant discomfort and unfamiliarity, not to mention having to go back to square one again.

Later, as they looked back, they realized they should've gotten out sooner. Sometimes we don't know until we know, but other times we let ourselves drift—and not to beat a dead horse, but *at this stage of life, how much time do you really have* to figure out if this person is a good match for you?

By the same token, we've met people who moved in with a new partner too quickly, and then had to face another break-up.

We can't emphasize enough the value of gut checks. Request regular meetings with it, ask it to report in. The decision to stay or go can be complicated—you don't want to make a rash decision, yet you don't want to linger too long, either. Any way you cut it, dating later in life is an intense process. Not for sissies.

Red Flags, Part Two

OK, so you've had a few dates, maybe more, with someone you met through an online dating site and are slowly realizing they don't have any friends or family, they act all mysterious about how and where they spend their time, or they have weird rules about when you can call them or when they're available for dates.

So you start asking questions. They have reasonable-sounding answers. You try to be trusting rather than suspicious. Then you catch them in a lie. They explain it away, but your gut is queasy.

They might be scammers, they might be married, but at the very least, they have a secret. Between the gut signals and all the red flags hitting you in the head by now, you probably should get the heck out of there.

"Can I Break Up by Text?"

Breaking up sucks. There are slim to no ways to do it without hurt feelings somewhere. Nobody likes to be on either end of rejection, and we twist ourselves into pretzels trying to figure out the easiest way to end things. Sometimes it's simpler to drift along, trying to convince ourselves it's all fine or good enough, rather than bite the bullet and admit it's not working. Then you look up, a year has gone by, and guess what? You're older and now you have to take new photos and....

It can be tempting to either ghost somebody as a way out or send them a sensitive-sounding (you hope) text that gets you out scott-free. There's no definitive right or wrong here but maybe we need a new Miss Manners to help us all deal with the rules of cyber-communication. In general, the more emotionally involved and long-term the relationship, the more texting, as a way to say goodbye, is so wrong.

Don't be a weenie.

Breaking up well requires nerve and courage, but it can be done. You might end up with a friendship afterward. Both Debi and I, as well as other men and women we've talked to, have developed friendships with some dates that didn't turn into romances. But you need to have that adult conversation, the kind where nobody yells and says stupid things or stomps away into the night.

Sometimes the break-up doesn't go well, but after a bit of time has passed, you can reconnect and at least part as friends. Debi came to regret how she broke up with a man she dated for a while and so she sent him a text to apologize. He was relieved to hear from her, and they were able to talk about what had happened in a much different way. Maybe they'll be friends, maybe not. But they both felt much better about themselves and each other afterward.

Oh and don't forget—after being together for a while, some of your stuff is going to be at their house and some of theirs will be at yours. If you don't break up well, you might lose that stuff, so figure this in to your departure scenario.

I have a friend who'd been seeing a woman for a little while but then met another woman he liked much more. He did that "slip out the back, Jack" thing with the first woman, hoping he could get away with ghosting as a method of breaking up.

After a few weeks of not hearing from him, she texted him to say she guessed it was over, but she'd like some closure and asked him to stop over for a face-to-face. He was sweating bullets over the prospect of having to break up in person. He agonized over what to say.

When he finally came back from visiting her, he stood there looking sheepish and holding a lamp he'd lent her. He said the conversation had gone well, and she was fine and he was fine, it was over and he was relieved. I admired her for making closure happen and being the adult in the room. And for giving his lamp back. Not everyone would.

Quitting When There's Chemistry

We should've added "sex organs" to the list of talking body parts, because they definitely weigh in when we're making decisions about whether to keep the relationship going. "But I'm attracted to him/her; that must mean something."

Chemistry can convince us we've got a relationship worth saving. We walk away when it's not there, though the person may be quite compatible—other times the relationship is crappy but we stay because there's chemistry. You'd think we'd all have figured this stuff out by this age, but no.

Chemistry feels amazing and gets confused with love. But attraction and lust are not enough to make a relationship. It makes us tingle, but if the relationship isn't working except for the chemistry, hopefully the rest of your body parts will overrule the sex parts and you'll be able to move on.

Once you do, however, beware of those lonely nights when your fingers are itching to send a little message to someone you remember fondly. We call this maneuver the "circle back," when you try again with someone you dated a while ago. Men who trust us have admitted that, for them, the circle back move is more about sex, while women who circle are more focused on a new, improved relationship. Are we surprised?

This whole question of when to stay and when to go or circle back led Debi and me to a discussion about how you decide if this is the one you want to stick with. Will it be startlingly obvious, or a deliberate decision arrived at after weighing all the baggage, emotions, chemistry, values, and lifestyles? I've been carrying around this version of "knowing" from my younger self, when exploding fireworks, butterflies in the stomach, and a complete loss of common sense left no room for doubt.

I talked to a therapist who said, "It's different when you're older. It might not feel like that." This was something I'd never considered. I thought true love always felt the same way, and then they tell me the old compass isn't reliable anymore.

Finding that Last First Date

> "You're only like eight horribly
> toxic relationships away from
> finding your soulmate."
>
> — Author Unknown

Finding "It"

HERE'S A SWEET little story to let you know what you might experience if you give this dating thing a try:

Debi and I attended a small dinner party a while ago. We were all sitting out on the patio enjoying wine and potluck appetizers, and watching the sun dip into the ocean, except for one guy, who'd been divorced a couple of years. He was smiling down at his phone.

"Excuse me a minute. I gotta take this," he said, and bolted away into the house.

He was over sixty years old, but he looked like an eighteen-year-old in puppy love. Every time before when I'd seen him since his divorce, he looked grim and serious. His most often-repeated sentiment, spoken with stoic resignation was, "I had many good years of marriage. I don't think at this age I'll fall in love again." He sometimes scoffed at me because I believed it was possible.

The party was made up of a group of close friends, many married but more than a few of us recently single. I noticed that all the single people had our phones out, either in our hands or nearby and visible. We were constantly checking screens, and either smiling and typing, or looking anxious. The married people's phones were nowhere to be seen.

Eventually my friend returned. There was no mistaking the boyish grin on his face.

"Are you in love?" I teased him.

"I don't know. It's too soon. But I didn't think I could feel this way again, and I'm just so glad that I can." And with that, another text came in from her, and he was gone.

Brené Brown, PhD, LMSW and author of the book *The Gifts of Imperfection,* developed a definition of love, based on her research:

"We cultivate love when we allow our most vulnerable and powerful selves to be deeply seen and known, and when we honor the spiritual connection that grows from that offering with trust, respect, kindness, and affection.

Love is not something we give or get; it is something that we nurture and grow, a connection that can only be cultivated between two people when it exists within each one of them—we can only love others as much as we love ourselves.

Shame, blame, disrespect, betrayal, and the withholding of affection damage the roots from which love grows. Love can only survive these injuries if they are acknowledged, healed, and rare."

Debi and I came up with our own list of characteristics for a good relationship. We tried to keep it short and simple, to avoid falling into the "perfection" trap. In the end, however, when you know, you know. Lists come from the head, love comes from the heart.

- They "get" you and you "get" them, including each other's sense of humor. (They don't give you those "What the fuck are you talking about?" looks all the time.)

- You feel easy and comfortable when you're together (not walking on eggshells, and you can go back to wearing that comfy sweatshirt sometimes)

- You accept each other's weaknesses and imperfections, fears and anxieties

- You feel good about yourself in the relationship

- Your sex life is mutually fulfilling

- The spark between you maintains over time, and transforms from simple chemistry into a deep connection of love and affection

- You can talk about difficult subjects and differences calmly and lovingly (well, most of the time. Or at least you can come back and apologize and start over if you screwed up).

Hopefully, this list is not too much to expect. We're not saying it should be like this 100% of the time. How about most of the time? OK, some of the time?

This list covers the yummy stuff, the love stuff. Once you find that and you decide to make a life together, you have to figure out where to put everyone's baggage. Geographic distance? Still raising children? Busy in a career? Money issues? Health problems? Issues with families? Then there are the questions of marriage, living together, or living separately.

If you get too overwhelmed with all these questions of what a relationship is, or should be, or could be, the words of American spiritual teacher and author Ram Dass might help:

"In the end we are all just walking each other home."

And your journey begins...

In Closing

☐ *Single*
☐ *In a relationship*
☐ *Who cares? I'm awesome.*

*S*O PEOPLE, THIS is where we leave you. We hope this little refresher has helped you in some meaningful ways to figure out how to date again, do it with a bit of confidence, and ponder those eternal questions about life and love and aging and death that plague us all.

Oh yeah, and maybe you'll find love again. We really, really hope so.

For more, join us at www.datingafterfifty.com

Appendix

The profiles and excerpts in this section are lifted directly from online dating sites. Some need a complete make-over, others need some tweaking to bring out the personality and others we found effective.

Seriously Problematic Profiles

The following list of profiles are not excerpts, but complete statements written by a person seeking a romantic partner. We provide them as examples of what NOT to do.

- I'm (sic) skinny guy, I like white skinny women
- I like to do a lot of things or nothing at all
- Fun and loving
- Music, reading. Knowledge about a lot of subjects

- I am a person who does not like to be lied, to be cheated on or to be used, so for a start if that's what you are after then don't bother because I will not give you the time of the day. Other than that I consider myself to be a man with a great sense of humor and funny.

- I really hate talking about myself. I think eye contact is a must [while wearing sunglasses in his profile photo]

- I have a good way to communicate with people

- I'm alone and want company

- I'm looking for someone who would like to be in a relationship with someone

- Easy to please, not a hold (sic) digger, not extravagant, not a material girl, So much more

Generic Profiles

The following excerpts from online profiles are reasonably descriptive but could be much better. Words in bold indicate places where being more specific would make the profile more interesting and personal.

- Recently retired in search of that special someone. Love the beach, **family** and **travel** to **warm** or **interesting places**.

- Like to **travel**, go on cruises, attend **sporting events**, go to **concerts**, I like the **ocean**, Hawaii, some gambling.

- Tall, slender, good listener, **storyteller**, **curious**, **empathetic**.

- Have a good heart and **care** about others. Like **most activities** and looking for someone to share **good times** with.

- I love **new experiences**, **good** food, wine, and great **conversation**. I love to garden and I love the **outdoors**.

Canned Profiles Supplied by Some Dating Site Somewhere

These are full profile suggestions by a dating site. Not only are they lame, but if you use one, your "profile" will be repeated by others who use the same service and you'll sound like a clone.

- I think I'm pretty easy to get along with. I think it's because I like to listen as much as I like to talk. People find it easy to communicate with me and I think that's a big reason why.

- Call me an optimist, but I tend to believe that things will work, no matter how bad. My positive outlook has helped me get through a lot of challenges.

- Some people call me spontaneous, but I just like to keep things open. Because sometimes that's when the truly special moments happen.

Profiles More Likely to Grab Your Attention

These are excerpts from humorous profiles we liked, and that tell you some important things about the person while being funny.

- I enjoy going out to dinner and eating meals that I will never figure out how to make myself. I also like martinis. After one, I'm very relaxed and at ease…after two, I think I'm the funniest human being on earth…if I ever have a third one, I'll be sound asleep within 12 minutes.

- May our baggage fit into each other's overhead compartment.

- My idea of roughing it is no mint on my hotel pillow.

- I'm looking for someone to drive me crazy and keep me sane.

- 5'10", 165–168 lbs, depending on how many cookies I've had.

- Let's be honest. The first thing we all look at is the pictures, and sadly mine are not the best. On the upside, I still have a full head of hair and can see my feet clearly.

- Hello. Let's get the important things out of the way first: I trim my nose hair, lift and put down the toilet seat, use GPS or ask directions, loved my mother, pick up clothes, consider belittling a female partner a hanging offense, clean bathrooms, do my own laundry, and never posed shirtless nor with a car, motorcycle, or in a hat.

Romantic Profiles

These excerpts demonstrate what the writer hopes to give in a romantic relationship. We like these more than ones that focus on what *you* can do for *me*.

- You want to be in my arms as much as I want you in mine.

- Any woman brave enough to choose me is guaranteed a wonderful, memorable evening either dining and dancing or eating popcorn and binge-watching Game of Thrones. Your call. As long as you're there, I'm down with it.

- I don't have many firsts left, but I'd like to find someone I could offer all my lasts.

- I will find you magically delicious, I'll stash little notes where you least expect to find them, I'll cover you up and kiss your forehead.

- Spending time being close to you makes me happy.

- I love your touch, your voice....

- To come home after being apart, and see the smile on your face, Wow!

Overused Phrases

So now it's time to write your own profile. To save you some time, here is a list of some of the most overused phrases in online dating profiles. Avoid them if you want to stand out from the crowd.

Hand in hand

Walks on the beach

I'm an optimistic person

Love to laugh

Love my family

Love my friends

Authentic, caring

Anything with sunsets or beaches

Kind, considerate, compassionate, fun

Positive attitude

No baggage

No drama

Anything about snuggling or cuddling on a couch

Passionate about life

Active

I like going out

Have a good sense of humor

Love to travel

Love music

Live life to the fullest

Netflix (what's with all the Netflix, people? Face it, you like to watch TV!)

Made in the USA
Las Vegas, NV
20 November 2020

11217069R00098